A Student's Guide to

ARTHUR
MILLER

Amy Dunkleberger

Enslow Publishers, Inc.

40 Industrial Road	PO Box 38
Box 398	Aldershot
Berkeley Heights, NJ 07922	Hants GU12 6BP
USA	UK

http://www.enslow.com

Library of Congress Cataloging-in-Publication Data

Dunkleberger, Amy.
    A student's guide to Arthur Miller / Amy Dunkleberger.
        p. cm. — (Understanding literature)
    Includes bibliographical references and index.
    ISBN 0-7660-2432-6
    1. Miller, Arthur, 1915–2005—Criticism and interpretation—Handbooks,
manuals, etc.—Juvenile literature. I. Title. II. Series.
    PS3525.I5156Z627 2005
    812'.52—dc22
                                 2004029125

Printed in the United States of America

10 9 8 7 6 5 4 3 2 1

To Our Readers:
We have done our best to make sure all Internet addresses in this book were active
and appropriate when we went to press. However, the author and the publisher
have no control over and assume no liability for the material available on those
Internet sites or on other Web sites they may link to. Any comments or suggestions
can be sent by e-mail to comments@enslow.com or to the address on the back cover.

Illustration Credits: AP/Wide World Photos.

Cover Illustration: AP/Wide World Photos (inset); Corel Corporation/
Hemera Technologies, Inc. (background objects).

CONTENTS

EVERY MAN'S PLAYWRIGHT

An introduction to the life and works of Arthur Miller

> Plays leave a wake behind them as they pass into
> history, with odd objects bobbing about in it. [1]
>
> —Arthur Miller

Between his first play, the 1947 hit *All My Sons*, and his last in 2004, Arthur Miller, one of the great American playwrights of the twentieth century, has left behind a considerable wake. With each new generation of theatergoers, Miller's plays are rediscovered. *Death of a Salesman* (1949) has been performed countless times in countless languages. *The Crucible* (1953) has enjoyed repeated interpretations on stage, television, and film, in countries around the world. *After the Fall* (1964) and *The Price* (1968) continue to be revived. And up until his death in early 2005, Miller kept producing new work, year after year.

With *All My Sons, Death of a Salesman,* and *The Crucible,* Miller brought a challenging perspective to the theater, one that dared audiences both to think and feel. Molded by the Great Depression, World War II, and America's war on Communism, Miller established himself early on as a writer of important social plays. Decades later his attention to history remains strong.

As Miller biographer Martin Gottfried noted in 2003:

> He has grappled with the world around him in an almost athletic way, as though his life span were game time and current history the arena. He thrived there, having participated in most of the twentieth century's crucial events—the Wall Street crash of 1929, the Great Depression, the socialist movement, the birth of organized labor. In one sense or another his life touched upon the rise of Nazism in Europe, America's emergence as a world power following the Second World War, juvenile delinquency in America, racial and religious prejudice, the development of world communism, the birth of the Atomic Age, the cold war, the anticommunism of the McCarthy era and the Vietnam war years with their social and political reverberations.[2]

As a young artist, Miller was inspired by ancient Greek theater and the works of nineteenth-century Norwegian dramatist Henrik Ibsen and Russian novelist Fyodor Dostoyevsky. Over time, he developed his craft and found his voice—his own style of storytelling. In addition to playwriting, Miller produced fiction, screenplays, an autobiography, a children's book, essays, and other nonfiction. Miller wrote volumes about the art of playwriting and rigorously examined his own works.

As with all artists, Miller's work is a reflection of his life. He often found inspiration in his past, and many of his personal experiences are dramatized in his plays. *A Memory of Two Mondays* (1955), for example, depicts Miller's days as a young clerk in a Depression-era auto-parts warehouse. The financial ruin of Miller's father, a Brooklyn, New York, factory owner who lost his fortune when Miller was a teenager, is described in one of his later plays, *The American Clock* (1980). In *After the Fall* (1964) Miller scrutinizes his failed marriages to his first wife, Mary, and movie star Marilyn Monroe. *Finishing the Picture* (2004) draws on his experiences as a reluctant screenwriter.

What makes Miller's dramatic writing timeless, however, is his understanding of human emotions, emotions like jealousy, shame, fear, love, lust, hate, and envy. Without them his plays might read like the editorial page of a newspaper. Instead, Miller dramatizes how emotions intersect with social issues and become the basis of history. In a 2003 magazine interview, Miller stated, "A play should be written about something the playwright feels passionate about. You look for the artist's soul, not the day's news."[3]

COMMON THEMES

Morality

Although Miller writes in a number of formats and styles, certain themes dominate his major dramatic works. First and foremost is the theme of right and wrong, the how and why of morality. In the press preview of *All My Sons*, Miller wrote: "In all my plays and books I try to take settings and dramatic situations from life which involve real questions of right and wrong. Then I set out, rather implacably and in the most situations I can find, the moral dilemma and try to point a real, though hard, path out."[4]

Guilt

Miller considers conscience—and its complement, guilt—on both a social and personal level. Sometimes called problem plays, many of his dramas examine how choices made by the individual reflect and influence society. In plays such as *All My Sons*, *An Enemy of the People* (1950), *The Crucible*, *A*

View from the Bridge (1956), *Incident at Vichy* (1964), and *Resurrection Blues* (2001), Miller compels his protagonists to choose between their personal needs and the needs of society.

In other plays Miller examines how conscience affects his characters on a private and familial level. *Death of a Salesman*, *After the Fall*, *The Price*, and *Mr. Peter's Connections* (1998), for example, feature characters torn by guilt about their personal failings.

Family

Family, especially as seen in father-son and brother-brother relationships, is another favorite Miller theme. His play *The Creation of the World and Other Business* (1972) chronicles the ups and downs of Western literature's very first family—Adam, Eve, Cain, and Abel. Fathers and sons are at the core of *All My Sons* and *Death of a Salesman*. The father-son relationship is the dramatic center of *The Price*, even though the father is long dead and never appears on stage.

Dead, "ghost" family members often play a pivotal role in Miller's stories, driving characters' guilt and desires. In keeping with the theme of family, many of Miller's plays, such as *All My Sons*, take place in and around a single house. Moral dilemmas may push the action of Miller's dramas, but families provide their foundation.

Self-discovery

Self-discovery is yet another theme in Miller's work. As Miller noted in his foreword to *After the Fall*, "The apple cannot be stuck back on the Tree of Knowledge; once we begin to see, we are doomed and challenged to seek the strength to see more, not less."[5] The conflict in Miller's plays is often a struggle between knowledge and ignorance, truth-telling and secrecy.

A long-held secret lies at the heart of *All My Sons* and *Death of a Salesman*, and in many of Miller's later plays—*After the Fall, Danger: Memory!* (1987), *The Ride Down Mt. Morgan* (1991), and *Broken Glass* (1994), for example—the main characters engage in exhaustive self-examination and truth-seeking. For Miller the process of unmasking the truth is as fascinating as the truth itself.

Common Characters

Conveying Miller's themes are strong, distinctive characters. Willy Loman, the doomed central character of *Death of a Salesman*, is one of the most memorable figures of the twentieth-century stage. Willy has come to symbolize America's "little man"— an ordinary father and husband. John Proctor, the flawed protagonist of *The Crucible*, who was based on a real-life Salem, Massachusetts, farmer, reminds

Arthur Miller is pictured here standing outside a New York theatre some time in 1950.

audiences of all the courageous individuals who have fought against repression.

In their outlook and experiences most of Miller's characters are uniquely American, but in their dreams and fears they are universal. Miller preferred writing about the working and middle classes—the type of people he grew up and went to school with. His characters are businessmen, mechanics, carpenters, farmers, dockworkers, clerks, and lawyers. They are Jewish, Catholic, and Protestant, New Englanders, Midwesterners, and New Yorkers.

SYMBOL—*Something that stands for, represents, or suggests another thing.*
SYMBOLISM—*The representation of things by use of symbols.*

Not surprisingly, Miller's most effective and significant characters are men. Women often supply the moral core of his stories, but men act out the moral dilemma. The men usually represent two generations, two eras in combat with each other. Only a few are heroic. Most are flawed and confused—ordinary men in extraordinary circumstances.

MILLER'S THEATER

Structure and Style

Plays differ from novels and short stories in that the bulk of the narrative is conveyed through character dialogue, not through descriptions and character thoughts (interior monologue). While the action of the story can be set anywhere and can jump around in time, as it can in fiction, the presentation of a drama unfolds within a definite period, usually two to three hours.

A playwright's voice is a combination of dialogue and stage directions. To help tell their stories, playwrights describe sets, props, lighting, costumes, and music, although stage directors sometimes change or drop these theatrical devices for a given production. Plays can be appreciated through silent reading alone, but their full impact can be experienced only through an actual production, with actors and staging.

Structurally, plays are unique. Sometimes they are divided into distinct blocks called scenes and acts. Scenes are small sections, like chapters in a novel. They usually take place within a continuous time frame and in one location, with characters entering and exiting. Acts are longer, sometimes containing many scenes.

Over the centuries the number of acts typically seen in a drama has changed. During William Shakespeare's time five-act plays were the norm. Three-act plays, with three curtains and two intermissions, became popular in the first half of the twentieth century. The three-act structure, which was also adopted by movie writers, is sometimes referred to as classic structure. Today's dramas usually contain only two acts, with or without intermissions. Sometimes plays are written as a series of scenes, with no distinct act breaks.

Throughout his career Miller experimented with theatrical style and structure, selecting the mode of storytelling he believed best suited a particular idea or character. "[M]y own tendency has been to shift styles according to the nature of my subject. . . . This in order to find speech that springs naturally out of the characters and their backgrounds rather than imposing a general style."[6]

In his first two produced plays—*The Man Who Had All the Luck* (1945) and *All My Sons*—Miller relied on conventional dramatic structure and style to tell his story. Both plays have three acts and advance their narrative in a straightforward manner. The characters speak naturalistically—that is, they use phrasing and expressions common to their age, where they are from, and their social status. The passage of time is chronological and clearly presented.

With *Death of a Salesman*, Miller abandoned the three-act structure and experimented with dreamlike stage devices. Lighting, in particular, became a key component of the narrative. Actions within scenes were no longer chronological, but jumped back and forth in time.

REALISM

Despite these changes, Miller considered *Death of a Salesman* and many of his later plays to be as realistic as his first plays. In general, realistic plays, like other forms of realistic art, represent things as they actually are, or were. For Miller any drama "representing real rather than symbolic or metaphysical persons and situations" is realistic, regardless of how the characters speak or what the set looks like.[7] Poetry and dreams have a place in Miller's realism as long as they spring from the emotions of everyday life. Miller's biblical play *The Creation of the World and Other Business*, however, is nonrealistic because the characters and their actions are symbols representing all of mankind, not actual people or situations.

> **REALISM**—*In literature, a manner of treating subject matter that presents a careful, accurate description of everyday life.*

LANGUAGE

The language of a play, its dialogue, is its heart. In a magazine interview Miller once commented that playwriting is "an auditory experience. That's the difference between the novelist and the playwright. The novelist sees the work, the playwright hears it."[8] Whether he is writing about Italian Americans in Brooklyn or farmers in the Midwest, Miller's speech is noteworthy for its authentic, regional flair. He resists making his characters sound like mouthpieces—characters who make speeches or spout poetry in an artificial way. Instead, he plays with patterns of everyday speech, emphasizing rhythms and phrases that set the drama in a particular place and suggest a character's personality and social class.

METAPHYSICAL— *Concerned with abstract thoughts or subjects; relating to a reality beyond what is perceived with the senses.*

The following excerpt from the opening of Miller's contemporary play *The Last Yankee* (1991) exemplifies Miller's theatrical language. The story takes place in a New England psychiatric hospital, where Frick and Leroy, whose wives are patients at the hospital, are meeting for the first time in the visiting area:

> FRICK, *pointing right*: Supposed to notify somebody in there?
> LEROY, *indicating left:* Did you give your name to the attendant?
> FRICK: Yes. 'Seem to be paying much attention, though.
> LEROY: They know you're here, then. He calls through to the ward.

FRICK, *slight pause:* Tremendous parking space down there. 'They need that for?
LEROY: Well a lot of people visit on weekends. Fills up pretty much.
FRICK: Really? That whole area?
LEROY: Pretty much.
FRICK: 'Doubt that. *He goes to the window and looks out. Pause.* Beautifully landscaped, got to say that for it.
LEROY: Yes, it's a very nice place. . . .
FRICK: My name's Frick.
LEROY: Hi. I'm Hamilton.
FRICK: Gladameetu. *Slight pause.* How do you find it here?
LEROY: I guess they do a good job. . . .
FRICK: Awful lot of colored, though, ain't there?
LEROY: Quite a few, ya.[9]

In this brief exchange Miller establishes some of the differences between his two male characters. Frick uses slang ("ain't") and drops words from the start of his sentences (" 'They need that for?" instead of "What do they need that for?"). These speech habits help define Frick as rough and unsophisticated. His use of the word "colored" hints at not only his prejudices but also his age, as that term was commonly used in the first half of the twentieth century. Leroy, on the other hand, speaks in complete sentences and uses proper English. He is, in fact, the younger and more educated of the two.

17

Miller noted that despite the natural feel of the dialogue in this play, the characters' speech is also stylized. "It sounds like real, almost like reported talk, when in fact it is intensely composed, compressed, 'angled' into an inevitability that seems natural but isn't."[10] In other words, the language of Miller's characters is ordinary but each word is carefully selected and put together to convey the story's conflicts. In this way Miller's dialogue approaches poetry and is not reportage.

BROADWAY- BOUND

Youthful influences and development of the artist

Because so much of Arthur Miller's drama is autobiographical, his art is intertwined with his life. To fully appreciate his art, it helps to know something of his life. To understand his life, you have to know something about the history he lived.

RICH BOY, POOR BOY

"Nobody can know Brooklyn, because Brooklyn is the world, and besides it is filled with cemeteries, and who can say he knows those people?"[1] Brooklyn, New York, is the area where Miller spent his youth. Although Miller lived in Connecticut for much of his adult life, he never lost his Brooklyn accent and always considered Brooklyn his spiritual home. His earliest days, however, were spent in another borough of New York City—Manhattan.

Born in upper Manhattan on October 17, 1915, at

the height of World War I, Arthur Asher Miller was the second child of Isadore and Augusta Miller. His brother, Kermit, was two years older, and his sister, Joan, almost seven years younger. Although functionally illiterate, his father was a successful women's clothing manufacturer—tall, fair, and handsome. By contrast, Miller's mother was petite, dark complexioned, and "cultured." Gussie played the piano, read voraciously, and attended plays and concerts. As a young boy, Miller lived in an upscale Manhattan apartment and was sometimes driven around by a chauffeur. In his autobiography, *Timebends*, Miller recalls his mother wearing "diamonds on her fingers, and she trails a silver fox across the floor."[2]

In late 1929, however, the New York stock market crashed, and America was plunged into a devastating financial depression. Like many Americans, Miller's father had invested heavily in the stock market, and lost most of the family's money. The now poor Millers were forced to move near relatives in Brooklyn, which at the time was semirural. Gone were Gussie's diamonds and fur. Instead, Miller wrote, his mother would shuffle about "in carpet slippers, sighing, cursing with a sneer on her lips, weeping suddenly and then catching herself, in the winters feeding the furnace with as scant a shovelful of coal as will keep it burning."[3]

These early memories of wealth and poverty are vital to understanding the foundations of Miller's work. Such plays as *Death of a Salesman, The Price, After the Fall,* and *The American Clock* echo Miller's experience with the Depression and demonstrate the stress that financial misfortunes create within families.

JUDAISM

Judaism is another important aspect of Miller's upbringing. Although his immediate family was not overly religious, the neighborhoods in which he lived were soaked in Jewish culture and tradition. In *Timebends*, Miller writes, "I was six the year I entered school, and I could not, myself, ever have heard an anti-Semitic remark. Indeed, had I thought about it at all, I would have imagined that the whole world was Jewish."[4]

As his world expanded, however, Miller began encountering anti-Jewish prejudice. In his novel *Focus* (1945) Miller explored the theme of anti-Semitism, and many of his post–World War II works, including *Incident at Vichy, Playing for Time* (1980), and *Broken Glass,* deal with aspects of Judaism and religious intolerance. Miller's moral outlook, his humanism, owes much to his Jewish roots and education.

21

COLLEGE DAYS

After graduating from high school in 1932, Miller, who had always been more interested in sports than academics, took a number of jobs and began saving money for college. He worked as a truck driver, a singer on a local radio program, and a warehouse clerk. Full-grown, he was tall and lanky, and dark like his mother. In later years his appearance would be compared to Abraham Lincoln's.

In 1934, despite mediocre grades, Miller gained admission to the University of Michigan. It was there that Miller discovered his love of playwriting and expanded his political activism. The university had "a serious respect for undergraduate writing efforts" and offered students a prestigious playwriting prize, the Hopwood Award, of which Miller won two during his four-year stay.[5]

Miller developed a close, long-term relationship with his playwriting mentor, Professor Kenneth Rowe. Rowe taught Miller about play construction and offered him encouragement when needed. Although none of Miller's college plays were produced professionally, they helped bring Miller to the attention of the commercial theater world following graduation.

With its diverse student body the university also proved to be a perfect environment for lively political discussion, stirring Miller's social awareness. Miller, who started college as a journalism major, worked as a reporter and editor for the campus newspaper. In an essay about his university days, Miller says, "I tell you true, when I think of the library I think of the sound of a stump speaker on the lawn outside, because so many times I looked up from what I was reading to try to hear what issue they were debating now. The place was full of speeches, meetings, and leaflets. It was jumping with Issues."[6]

THE REAL WORLD

In 1938, after receiving his degree in English literature, Miller returned to New York and joined the Federal Theater Project, turning down an offer to write screenplays in Hollywood. Initiated during the Depression by President Franklin D. Roosevelt, the Federal Theater Project employed and funded writers and other artists. As a Project member, Miller wrote radio plays while continuing to work on his stage plays. After the Project folded, Miller was hired to write plays for commercial radio, including the CBS network.

Miller married fellow Michigan student Mary Grace Slattery in 1940. Mary came from a conservative, midwestern Catholic family, and as Miller observed, "There was a deep shadow then over intermarriage between Jews and gentiles, and still deeper

Arthur Miller sits before his typewriter on May 2, 1949.

if the gentile was Catholic."[7] Miller soon became aware of Mary's family's critical attitudes toward Jews and their indifference toward the mounting unrest in Nazi Germany. At the time, many Americans did not want to become involved in the Nazi conflict, feeling that the plight of Jews in Europe was not their concern. Years later Miller dramatized this indifference, this reluctance towards positive social action, in several of his plays, most notably *The Crucible* and *Broken Glass*.

In his early adulthood Miller moved between two worlds—the world of blue-collar labor and the world of literature. In 1942, following America's entrance into World War II, Miller threw himself into writing patriotic war plays for the radio. At the same time, he took a job as a ship fitter's helper at the navy yard in Brooklyn. As with his other life experiences, his time in the shipyards, which were dominated by immigrant Italian Americans, inspired his playwriting as well as his politics. *A View from the Bridge*, which Miller first wrote as a short one-act and later turned into a full-length play, was based, in part, on his navy yard days.

While he was earning good money writing radio plays and had even worked on the screenplay for the war film *The Story of G.I. Joe* (1945), Miller continued writing his stage plays. His first nonfiction book,

Situation Normal, which was based on his research for *G.I. Joe*, was published that same year with help from wife Mary. In September 1944 his daughter Jane was born.

BROADWAY

Two months later, eight years after the completion of his first student play, Miller finally got a major stage production. The story of successful mechanic David Beeves and his hapless older brother, Amos, *The Man Who Had All the Luck* includes many of the themes associated with Miller. Although it won Miller the Theatre Guild National Award and was published in an anthology, the play closed after only six performances on Broadway and was not seen onstage again for many years.

Late in 1945 Miller, discouraged by his playwriting failures, published *Focus*, his first and only full-length novel. Reaction to the book was mixed, but it helped keep Miller's name in the New York press. Miller returned to playwriting and, determined to produce a Broadway hit, took his time. Two years and seven hundred pages later, *All My Sons* was ready for production.

CHAPTER 3

THEY WERE ALL MY SONS

Examining *All My Sons*, first stage success

Originally titled *The Sign of the Archer, All My Sons* is, according to Miller biographer Martin Gottfried, "virtually a guided tour of his past, present and future. In it are autobiographical aspects, elements of his early playwriting efforts, a new professionalism and sinew and signals of the mastery that lay ahead."[1] Directed by the influential Elia Kazan and starring Ed Begley, Beth Merrill, and Arthur Kennedy, *All My Sons* opened at New York's Coronet Theatre on January 20, 1947. As hoped, the production received rave reviews and won many awards. Miller's theatrical frustrations were finally over.

Miller attributed his inspiration for his first major play to his mother-in-law Julia Slattery. "She had unknowingly triggered that play when she gossiped about a young girl somewhere in central Ohio who had turned her father in to the FBI for having manufactured faulty aircraft parts during the war."[2]

Although Miller kept the midwestern setting of Julia Slattery's gossip, he changed the "young girl" into a thirty-two-year-old man named Chris Keller. The suspect factory owner, Joe Keller, resembles Miller's father, Isadore. Like Isadore, Keller is a large, uneducated man of sixty who went to work when he was ten and is now obsessed with business.

Miller eventually added a brother, Larry, the "ghost" family member. Larry and Chris are both reminiscent of Miller's older brother, Kermit. During World War II, Kermit enlisted in the army and was injured in the Battle of the Bulge, the war's deadliest and longest battle. Although he survived, Kermit returned home a different man, a "ghost" of his former confident, lively self.

PLOT AND STRUCTURE— THE CLASSIC THREE-ACT

As noted earlier, *All My Sons* is written in three acts. In his student plays and *The Man Who Had All the Luck*, Miller experimented with the three-act structure. With *All My Sons*, he perfected it.

In the first act of a three-act drama, the story's

foundation is laid. The main characters are introduced, and the major conflicts are set up. Of the three acts, the first act contains the most exposition, or backstory. In addition to telling the audience who the characters are and what their relationships are to one another, the first act reveals important facts about the characters' pasts.

ACT ONE—LAYING THE FOUNDATION

Act one of *All My Sons* opens shortly after the end of World War II, a Sunday morning in August in "the back yard of the Keller home in the outskirts of an American town."[3] Joe Keller and neighbor Dr. Jim Bayliss are reading the newspaper together. Miller describes the yard and house in some detail, noting that the two-story building "is nicely painted, looks tight and comfortable, and the yard is green with sod, here and there plants whose season is gone."[4] Downstage, Miller indicates, "stands the four-foot-high stump of a slender apple-tree whose upper trunk and branches lie toppled beside it, fruit still clinging to its branches."[5]

Another neighbor, Frank Lubey, drops by to chat and immediately notices the tree, which was wrecked by the previous night's windstorm. Frank, an amateur astrologer, comments on the coincidence of the tree toppling in the same month that Keller's son Larry was to turn twenty-seven. A military pilot during the war, Larry was shot down near China and declared missing in action. Although over three years have passed, Keller's wife, Kate, refuses to accept that her son has died and has asked Frank to do Larry's astrological chart.

Frank drills Keller about Larry's former fiancée and next-door neighbor, Ann Deever, who arrived at the Kellers' the night before, a guest of Larry's younger brother, Chris. Also curious about Ann are Jim's wife, Sue, and Frank's wife, Lydia. Keller is questioned, then teases Bert, a young boy from the neighborhood, about the "jail" in his cellar and the importance of maintaining "law and order" on the block.

Although these opening conversations seem inconsequential, they are actually a vital part of Miller's dramatic structure. Through them Miller establishes Keller as a seemingly well-liked fixture in the neighborhood, one whom others both enjoy and respect. They also introduce the Kellers' neighbors, characters who, while not active in the plot, comment on the action. They act, in effect, like society, extensions of the audience, and as foils to the play's action.

After the neighbors disperse, Chris reveals to Keller that he saw Kate weeping over the fallen tree.

Chris begs Keller to be honest with Kate about Larry. "Why shouldn't she dream of him?" he says. "Do we contradict her? Do we say straight out that we have no hope any more?"[6] Keller rejects Chris's suggestion, however, declaring that as long as "there's no grave," Kate will refuse to accept her son's death.[7]

Chris then admits the real reason he wants to settle the question of Larry's death: He has invited Ann to his home in order to propose to her. Although he last saw her when he went off to war five years before, he has been writing steadily to her, and "when I think of someone for a wife, I think of Annie."[8] Keller warns Chris that Kate will not accept the marriage as long as she believes that Larry is alive. Chris, who has been working at Keller's plant since leaving the military, threatens to move away with Ann if his parents refuse to support his decision to marry.

As though sensing what Chris intends, Kate enters and immediately begins praising Ann as Larry's faithful girlfriend. Although Chris meekly suggests that his mother bury Larry in her mind, she refuses, and once alone with her husband, she criticizes him for not backing her up.

Kate's outburst is interrupted by the entrance, at last, of Ann. Ann tries to keep the conversation light, but Kate can only talk about Larry. Like Chris, Ann is sure that Larry died when his plane went down. No, Kate says, he survived, and as long as he is alive, Ann must wait for him.

Just then, neighbor Frank returns and asks Ann about her father, Steve, who, it turns out, has been serving time in a nearby Ohio prison. During the war Steve, Keller's former business partner, was arrested for shipping defective airplane engine parts, which then caused a number of deadly crashes. Keller was also arrested but was eventually cleared and released.

Ann insists that she holds nothing against Keller, but Keller feels compelled to explain himself: "The story was, I pulled a fast one getting myself exonerated. . . . I was the beast; the guy who sold cracked cylinder heads to the Army Air Force; the guy who made twenty-one P-40s crash in Australia. . . . Except I wasn't, and there was a court paper in my pocket to prove I wasn't."[9]

To Keller's dismay, Ann connects her father's crime to Larry's disappearance, saying, "He knowingly shipped out parts that would crash an airplane. And how do you know Larry's wasn't one of them?"[10] Keller rejects Ann's conclusion that her father's actions led to the crash of Larry's plane, as the defective parts were used in a different model.

Finally alone, Ann accepts Chris's proposal and assures him that she is through grieving for Larry.

Chris then admits that he is still haunted by the selfless men who died under his command during the war. "They didn't die," he explains, "they killed themselves for each other."[11] After Chris also confesses that he feels guilty about his postwar prosperity, he and Ann vow to tell Kate about their engagement.

Before they can, however, Keller interrupts them to announce that Ann's brother, George, is calling from Columbus, Ohio, where Steve is serving time in prison. Like Ann, George has been living in New York and until that moment had cut all ties with his father. To Ann's surprise, George announces that he is leaving Columbus right away to see her.

Privately Kate worries about why George, a lawyer, suddenly agreed to visit his father and why he is insisting on seeing Ann at the Kellers'. Although Keller maintains he has nothing to hide from George, Kate advises him to "be smart. The boy is coming. Be smart."[12]

Act one ends on this note of tension and mystery. Chris is still keeping his plan to marry a secret from Kate. Kate and Keller have been keeping their own secret, a secret they fear will soon be revealed. The past, they sense, has finally caught up to them and is threatening to upend their peaceful life.

ACT TWO—TURNING UP THE HEAT

To be successful, the second act of a three-act play must keep the suspense of the first act going while building to the inevitable conclusion of the third act. The resolution of the story's conflict cannot come too soon, however. The characters must test one another, advancing and retreating as they do battle. By the end of the second act, all avenues, physical and psychological, must be explored until only one possible course for the characters remains.

Act two of *All My Sons* begins a few hours after act one. Outwardly, the Kellers and Ann are preparing to go out for dinner. Emotionally, however, they are preparing for George's arrival from Columbus. Still in an agitated state, Kate complains to Chris, "To his last day in court Steve never gave up the idea that Dad made him do it."[13] Chris, trusting in his father's goodness, tries to reassure his mother about George and, by extension, Keller.

Keller then suggests to Ann that if her father were to take a job with him upon his release, he would be less likely to resent Chris and demand Ann's loyalty. Despite Ann's reassurances, Keller is convinced that if forced to choose, Chris would sever ties with his own father, a fate he could not endure.

"My only accomplishment is my son," he protests. "I ain't brainy. That's all I accomplished."[14]

Finally George arrives, and the dreaded showdown begins. George announces to Chris and Ann that after visiting his father in prison, he is now convinced that Keller lied about the cylinder heads and pinned the blame on Steve. Keller, he says, hid at home after Steve called with the news that their machinery was producing cracked engine parts. Instead of ordering a shutdown, Keller instructed Steve to cover the cracks and ship the cylinders.

Although Ann and Chris refuse to accept George's conclusions, George argues that "the same man who knows how many minutes a day his workers spend in the toilet" would have been aware of what Steve was doing.[15] George accuses Keller of ruining the Deever family and demands that Ann leave with him that day.

George then confronts Keller directly. Keller denies all of George's charges, getting George to admit that Steve, a "little man," often blamed others for his mistakes. George is about to give Keller the benefit of the doubt when Kate inadvertently mentions that Keller has not been sick in fifteen years. During Steve's trial Keller claimed to have been sick with the flu when Steve called him from the factory.

Kate tries to retract her statement, but George sees through her denials.

Finally, Keller is forced to admit to Chris that he did, in fact, order Steve to cover up the defect in the cylinder heads and lied about it at his trial. Keller insists that he lied only to protect his family and the business he worked so hard to build. Chris rejects all of Keller's arguments, screaming, "Don't you have a country? Don't you live in the world?"[16] Overwhelmed by the truth, Chris storms away. On this dramatic note the curtain falls on act two.

ACT THREE—THE END OF THE ROAD

As is typical in three-act dramas, the final act of *All My Sons* is considerably shorter and faster paced than the first two. All of the problems of the play have been presented; the characters have been challenged. In the last act conflicts are resolved, for better or worse. Their resolution is inevitable but not necessarily predictable.

Act three picks up hours after act two, in the middle of the night. Chris is still gone, and confused by his anger, Keller declares to Kate that "I'm his father and he's my son, and if there's something bigger than that I'll put a bullet in my head!"[17] Keller insists that unlike the more idealistic Chris, Larry would have understood why he lied.

Determined to save her relationship with Chris, Ann then makes a bargain with Keller and Kate: She will keep quiet about Keller's crime if Kate admits to Chris that Larry is dead. When Kate refuses, Ann shows her a letter that Larry wrote to her just before he went missing. Kate reads the letter silently and is dumbstruck. Chris then returns and, unaware of the letter, announces that he cannot bring himself to turn his father in.

As Kate struggles to stop her, Ann hands Larry's letter to Chris. With growing dread, Chris reads it out loud, revealing the final, horrible truth about Keller's deed: Upon learning about his father's arrest in the newspapers, Larry, overwhelmed with shame, decided to crash his airplane during his next mission. "Every day," Larry wrote, "three or four men never come back and he sits back there doing business."[18]

Realizing that Larry committed suicide because of him, a remorseful Keller declares that he is ready to serve his time in prison, and a still angry Chris offers to drive him to the police station. When Kate tries to dissuade her husband by pointing out that Larry was his son too and would not have wanted him to go to jail, Keller says, "Sure, he was my son. But I think to him they were all my sons."[19]

37

Keller then walks off, and a gunshot rings out. In that moment Kate, Ann, and Chris understand that like Larry, Keller has taken his own life. Feeling responsible, Chris begs his mother's forgiveness, but Kate beseeches him not to burden himself with his father's deeds. As Kate sobs, the final curtain falls.

THEMES

Although *All My Sons* operates on many levels, the center of its conflict is social. The Kellers and their neighbors represent the greater community, and the play depicts the community's struggle between self-sacrifice and self-preservation.

Miller wrote about the play:

> The fortress which *All My Sons* lays siege to is the fortress of unrelatedness. It is an assertion not so much of a morality in terms of right and wrong, but of a moral world's being such because men cannot walk away from certain of their deeds. In this sense Joe Keller is a threat to society and in this sense the play is a social play.[20]

Keller's need to protect his business and his family is at odds with society's need for sacrifice during wartime. Miller dramatizes how Keller, by putting himself first, betrayed not only Steve but his community as well.

In addition to the story told by his mother-in-law,

"It was a madhouse. Every half hour the Major callin' for cylinder heads, they whippin' us with the telephone. The trucks were hauling them away hot, damn near. I mean just try to see it human, see it human."[21]

That's how factory owner Keller describes his time as an aircraft parts manufacturer during World War II.

Audiences who first saw *All My Sons*, which opened less than two years after the war, would have immediately understood Keller's predicament. In December 1941, following the Japanese's attack on Pearl Harbor in Hawaii, President Franklin D. Roosevelt declared war on Japan and Germany. In January 1942 he then unveiled an ambitious plan for arming the military and established the War Production Board (WPB) to oversee construction. In addition to 120,000 tanks, Roosevelt ordered that 60,000 new airplanes be built in 1942 and 125,000 more in 1943.

The plan was particularly demanding because in 1941 America was still recovering from the Depression and overall manufacturing levels were low. In 1940, for example, the United States had only forty-one airplane engine and propeller factories, but by 1943 the number had increased to eighty-one. In 1944 a total of 96,379 airplanes were built, as compared to only 5,865 in 1939.

To complete the massive construction job, the U.S. government hired over six hundred thousand manufacturing contractors and many more subcontractors. Some contractors, like Miller's fictional Joe Keller, converted existing factories in order to build new types of equipment. Businessmen were paid well for their contributions but were expected to turn out product at a fast clip or risk losing their contracts.

In the early 1940s a Congressional committee, headed by Harry S. Truman, then a senator from Missouri, investigated abuses and problems in wartime rationing and manufacturing. As the character Keller reveals, the pressure to work quickly sometimes led to faulty products. A decision such as Keller's to cover up a fault in order to protect a government contract was deemed not only criminally negligent but unpatriotic. When caught, the guilty were severely punished.

Miller found inspiration for the play in interviews he conducted with soldiers while researching the script for *The Story of G.I. Joe* (which in 1945 he turned into his first book, *Situation Normal*). Miller was particularly moved by the plight of a soldier named Watson, a decorated war hero struggling to find his place back home.

Miller noted how connected to his fellow soldiers Watson had felt and, by contrast, how unconnected he felt once at home. "Watson must return to his former group. He must reassume its little prejudices, its hates, its tiny aims. . . . Now he must live unto himself, for his own selfish welfare."[22] Like Watson, Chris in *All My Sons* experienced the joy of men working and sacrificing together for a common, life-and-death goal.

This experience makes Chris especially critical of Keller's crime. In the end, Chris forces Keller to recognize the limitations of his "family first" philosophy when he declares, "Once and for all you can know there's a universe of people outside and you're responsible to it, and unless you know that, you threw away your son because that's why he died."[23] He condemns his father not only because his cover-up hurt soldiers but because he chose his family's worldly comforts over the lives of strangers willing to sacrifice themselves for the greater community, the family of man, "all my sons."

CHARACTERS

The characters who enact the themes of *All My Sons* represent both the idealistic and the practical. As a firsthand witness to the sacrifices of war, Chris is an idealist, a person who pursues high and noble principles. He feels uncomfortable with the material trappings of success—the houses, cars, and refrigerators that his father's factory affords him. Although his father warns him that "a man can't be a Jesus in this world,"[24] Chris insists on integrity and honesty.

Chris's idealism intensifies as the play progresses. In act one he appears tentative with his parents and Ann. By the end of Act Two, however, he explodes with rage against Keller and later demands that Kate face up to what her husband has done. In act three Chris's indignation is tempered by guilt. Although Chris continues to condemn his father, he knows that to some extent he "looked the other way" when it came to Keller's explanations about Steve. By not questioning his father, Chris realizes that he helped Keller perpetuate his crime.

While Chris is an idealist, Keller is practical. As Miller biographer Sheila Huftel notes, Keller literally stands for the world Chris has come back to, self-centered and unseeing."[25] Like many who worked their way out of the Depression, Keller understands the world only in terms of financial success and security. "A man among men," as Miller describes him at the beginning of the play, Keller commands respect and is a natural leader. He is not an evil man, just a half-blind one, and through the course of the play, his eyes are opened by the unfolding events. When he finally sees what he has done, the knowledge is more than he can endure and he kills himself.

Ann is both idealistic and practical. Neighbor Sue Bayliss calls Ann the "female version" of Chris. Because of her beliefs, Ann stopped speaking to her father after his conviction, a fact that disarms Keller. "A father is a father!" he cries.[26] On the other hand, Ann is willing to bury Keller's confession in order to save her relationship with Chris. In this way, she is practical.

Kate exemplifies many of the older female characters in Miller's plays. Like the biblical Eve in *The Creation of the World and Other Business*, Kate is a matriarch. She is devoted to her husband and believes in the family unit above all else. Though she has always known about her husband's crime, she is willing to keep it a secret.

Kate insists on Larry's survival not only because she loves him but because his death in a plane crash would destroy Keller and, by extension, the family. Even when the truth about Larry's suicide comes out, her instincts are not to condemn Keller, but to protect him. After Keller shoots himself, she turns to Chris, her last hope, and sobs, "Don't take it on yourself. Forget now. Live."[27] Miller makes it clear, however, that Chris will not forget.

MOTIFS

To enhance their stories, playwrights often use motifs—recurring ideas, symbols, forms, and so forth—in their texts. Motifs in plays can be expressed through dialogue—repeated phrases or images— through props and set pieces, or through bits of action performed by the actors.

The Kellers' idyllic suburban house, in back of which the entire story is played, is the most visible motif of *All My Sons*. Lovingly maintained, it represents the Kellers' achievement as a family—pride of ownership and commitment to the neighborhood. As theater scholar Tom Scanlon notes, the Keller house "is set in a half-public, half-private environment, one where the warmth, ease and love of family life is extended to encompass a larger area of society."[28]

The house also represents the materialism that plagues Keller and Kate. Home ownership is the center of the American dream, a social and economic concept that emerged after World War II. For Keller, his house, an outward symbol of his financial success, has become interchangeable with his family.

Larry's apple tree is another important visible motif in the play. In his stage directions Miller indicates in different scenes that the characters are to look at and touch the tree. On one level the tree, planted in Larry's honor, serves to remind survivors of war of Larry's sacrifice. On another level the tree recalls the emotional turmoil surrounding Larry's disappearance. Likewise, the aftermath of the windstorm, as seen in the tree's broken limbs, hints at the emotional storm threatened by Ann's arrival.

The jail references that pop up during the play's first act are a verbal motif. In context they are jokes, but they are also meant to foreshadow, or anticipate, the core conflict of the play. After Keller jokes about putting children in his pretend jail, neighbor

JUXTAPOSE—*To place side by side in order to make a point.*

Frank reminds him about his former employee, Steve, who is sitting in a real jail, doing time for Keller's crime. By juxtaposing the imaginary jail with the real jail, Miller makes the revelation about Keller's injustice that much more startling.

MILLER AND HENRIK IBSEN

All My Sons has been called Miller's most "Ibsenesque" play, and Miller himself acknowledged his predecessor's influence on the work.

The author of such plays as *A Doll's House* (1879) and *Hedda Gabler* (1890), Henrik Ibsen (1828–1906) is regarded by many as the father of modern drama. In addition to revolutionizing stage speech, Ibsen was one of the first playwrights to create psychologically believable, identifiable characters. For Miller, however, Ibsen's most significant contribution to drama lay in the way he used the past to explain the present.

As Miller noted in a 1957 essay, Ibsen took great pains to describe his characters' past in order to explain the troubles of their present. Miller used the same technique in the first act of *All My Sons*. "*All My Sons*," Miller wrote, "takes its time with the past, not in deference to Ibsen's method as I saw it then [1947], but because its theme is the question of actions and consequences, and a way had to be found to throw a long line into the past in order to make that kind of connection viable."[29]

The way that Miller found to bring the past alive in *All My Sons* was to have Ann and her brother, both of whom have been long absent from the Kellers' neighborhood, show up on their doorstep. Their arrival, which has been set in motion by the guilt-ridden Chris, forces Keller and Kate to recall their past actions. Speaking from the grave, the letter from Larry becomes another powerful "long line into the past," setting in motion the terrible final consequence.

CHAPTER 4

LIFE AND DEATH OF THE SALESMAN

Examining *Death of a Salesman*

In his biography of Miller, Martin Gottfried described the excitement that Miller's follow-up to *All My Sons* generated in the theatrical world: "A new play by Arthur Miller was news, and its being directed by Elia Kazan was even bigger news. This would surely be one of the major events of the 1948–1949 theater season."[1]

On February 10, 1949, *Death of a Salesman* had its premiere on Broadway. Directed by Kazan and starring Lee J. Cobb, Mildred Dunnock, and Arthur Kennedy, the play was an immediate hit. Audiences wept at the plight of Willy Loman and were mesmerized by Miller's and Kazan's daring theatrics. Not only did the play enjoy a long Broadway run, with 742 performances, it won a Pulitzer Prize and made Miller a household name in America.

BIRTH OF A SALESMAN

In his autobiography, *Timebends*, Miller recalled that the jumping-off point for *Death of a Salesman* was a conversation he had with his uncle, Manny Newman, whom he happened to bump into while in Boston for the opening of *All My Sons*. Even though Miller had not seen Manny or his grown son Buddy in some time, Manny's first words to Miller were not a greeting but the comment that Buddy was "doing very well. Then I saw a passing look of embarrassment on his face. . ."[2]

Miller surmised that Manny's rudeness arose out of his competitive feeling for Miller, but according to Miller, Manny knew that "he had lost the contest in his mind between his sons and me. An enormous welling sorrow formed in my belly as I watched him merge into the crowd outside."[3]

In *Timebends*, Miller described Manny, a traveling salesman, as a small, dark man with an outrageous imagination and an inflated view of himself and his family. "He was a competitor, at all times, in all things, and at every moment. My brother and I he saw running neck and neck with his two sons in some race that never stopped in his mind."[4] Miller's cousin

Buddy was athletic, while Buddy's younger brother, Abby, was a handsome womanizer with a penchant for stealing. Despite Manny's boast, neither Buddy nor Abby were especially successful as adults.

The Newman family, nonetheless, captured Miller's imagination. The fact that Manny apparently had committed suicide soon after his Boston meeting with Miller only added to his mystique. "By this time," Miller noted, "I had known three suicides, two of them salesmen."[5] Thus the plight of the American salesman, as personified in his uncle, became Miller's next creative undertaking.

PLOT AND STRUCTURE

Although the three-act, Ibsenesque *All My Sons* launched Miller's playwriting career, he was not content to duplicate its form and style in *Death of a Salesman*. Instead, Miller abandoned the linear structure of *All My Sons* in favor of a more fluid approach. In the introduction to his collected plays, Miller wrote: "The *Salesman* image was from the beginning absorbed with the concept that nothing in life comes 'next' but that everything exists together and at the same time within us."[6] In other words, Miller wanted to dramatize the human thought process, its mixing of the present with the past, the real with the imagined.

"The first image that occurred to me which was to

result in *Death of a Salesman* was of an enormous face . . . which would appear and then open up, and we would see the inside of a man's head. In fact, *The Inside of His Head* was the first title."[7] Over time the play became less fanciful, more realistic, but the notion of exploring the inner workings of a mind stayed with Miller.

The full title of the play is *Death of a Salesman: Certain Private Conversations in Two Acts and a Requiem.* Although it is longer than most modern dramas (productions usually run about three hours), Miller breaks the story into two basic parts, with one intermission. Except for the requiem—a short scene at the play's end—the play takes place within a twenty-four-hour period, night to night. To accommodate the fluidity of the narrative, Miller

REQUIEM—*A service, hymn, or dirge for the dead.*

limits the number of set changes. Most of the action takes place at the Lomans' house, either in the present or in Willy's past.

ACT ONE—THE HOMECOMING

As with *All My Sons*, act one opens in a house. Unlike the sprawling suburban house in *All My Sons*, however, this Brooklyn, New York, house is fragile and cramped, surrounded by apartments. The house's two-story interior is visible. Miller indicates that the three rooms depicted—two upper bedrooms and a downstairs kitchen—are sparsely furnished. The master bedroom, for example, contains only a bed, chair, and a shelf with an athletic trophy.

The play opens as Willy Loman, the "Salesman," returns home late one night, startling his wife, Linda. Laden with suitcases, the over-sixty Willy admits to Linda that he came back early from his sales trip because he was exhausted and kept veering his car off the road. When Willy tells Linda that he was dreaming and having "strange thoughts" while driving, Linda urges him to talk to Howard Wagner, his boss, about working closer to home.

Linda and Willy then discuss their sons, Biff and Happy. While Linda is delighted that the thirty-four-year-old Biff has returned home from the West, Willy complains about Biff's lack of drive and meager salary. Linda sticks up for Biff, who left home ten years before and has been drifting from job to job ever since, insisting that he is not lazy, just lost. Biff's homecoming prompts Willy to recall the 1928 Chevy he used to own, and he lapses into a happy memory about his sons.

In the boys' bedroom, meanwhile, Biff and Happy are awakened by their father's return. The young men worry that Willy has had another car accident, and Happy confides that lately Willy has been talking to himself, mostly about Biff.

Complaining that Willy is overly critical of him, Biff defends his decision to quit the business world in favor of outdoor work. At the same time, Biff admits he has doubts about his lifestyle and lack of financial success. The womanizing Happy, who works in a low-level position at a store, confesses that he, too, is lonely and dissatisfied with his life.

Then, for the first time in the play, Willy's past, his memories, come to life. In the memory Willy, just back from a sales trip, watches the teenage Happy and Biff (played by the same actors as in the present-day scenes) polishing the 1928 Chevrolet.

As they talk about sports and their high school, popular athlete Biff reveals that he stole a football from the gym locker room. Although Willy orders Biff to return the ball, he seems unconcerned about the theft. Willy boasts about his plans to start his own family business, bigger and better than their neighbor Uncle Charley's. Bursting with love and admiration, Biff promises to score a touchdown in Willy's honor during the upcoming championship game.

Bernard, Charley's son and Biff's studious class-mate, then appears and warns Biff that unless he studies for his math exam, he will flunk and not be allowed to graduate. Willy dismisses Bernard, bragging

51

that Biff has already been offered three athletic scholarships. Willy observes to Biff that Bernard is not "well liked" and therefore will not do well in the business world. "Be liked and you will never want," Willy declares.[8]

Still in the past, Willy and Linda go over the family budget. At first, Willy claims to have had a very profitable sales trip. When Linda asks for exact figures, however, Willy admits that he actually made little and had to work long hours. He then reveals his suspicions that he is not "well liked" and is, in fact, ridiculed by his buyers as fat and loud. The uncomplaining Linda gives Willy a pep talk, assuring him that he is a good provider—handsome, lively, and, above all, adored by his sons.

Willy's memory then gradually shifts away from his home to a hotel room in Boston. There Willy complains to a woman, a secretary at a firm he does business with, about how lonely he gets on the road. As she finishes dressing, The Woman jokes and flirts with Willy, her sometimes lover. After The Woman thanks Willy for giving her a pair of stockings, she disappears.

Willy's recollections then return to Linda as she is mending a pair of stockings in her kitchen. Willy shouts at Linda to stop, saying, "I won't have you mending stockings in this house!"[9] Willy's memory ends in a noisy rush of exchanges about Biff, his math test, and his stealing.

Willy is jerked back into the present when Happy and Charley, awakened by Willy's late-night shouting, enter the kitchen. Obviously concerned about his old friend and neighbor, Charley offers Willy a job at his business, but the prideful Willy rejects it.

Then while playing cards with Charley, Willy recalls his much older brother, Ben. Willy tells Charley that years before, the highly successful, globe-trotting Ben had offered him a job in Alaska, but that Willy had opted to stay in Brooklyn. When Willy becomes completely immersed in his memory of Ben and begins to mutter and ramble, Charley stomps off, confused.

In the past Willy begs the flamboyant Ben to tell him the secret of his success and admits his fears that he is a bad father. Ben has no answers for Willy, however, and instead praises him for raising "manly chaps."

In the present Linda catches Willy talking to himself in the backyard and tries to coax him back inside. Biff then sees what is happening and reacts to his father's mental problems with a mixture of concern and disgust. Linda defends Willy, noting that while not a great man, he is "a human being, and a terrible thing is happening to him. So attention must be paid.

He's not to be allowed to fall into his grave like an old dog. Attention, attention must be finally paid to such a person."[10]

Unmoved, Biff calls Willy a "fake" and reminds his mother that Willy threw him out of the house years before. Linda, disturbed by Biff's hostility, reveals that Willy has been trying to kill himself. First, Linda says, he deliberately crashed his car. Then Linda discovered a short rubber hose hidden behind the water heater, with an attachment for the heater's gas line. Willy had obviously constructed the pipe in order to asphyxiate himself with gas, Linda says.

Horrified, Biff vows to stay and find a steady job. Biff then comments that Willy, who has been forced to work on commission instead of receiving a salary, would be much happier as a carpenter than a salesman. Willy enters and, hearing Biff's remarks, berates him. To diffuse the tension, Happy steps in and lets slip that Biff is meeting his former employer, Bill Oliver, the next morning.

Biff admits he is planning to ask Oliver for a loan to start his own sporting goods line. After Happy eagerly offers to join him in the business, Biff's enthusiasm rises and ignites Willy's hopes. Forgetting his troubles, Willy starts giving Biff advice on how to act with Oliver and how much money to ask for.

Act one ends as the family finally heads for bed.

In the master bedroom Linda gently asks Willy what Biff has been holding against him all these years, but Willy changes the subject. Downstairs, Biff finds Willy's rubber tube behind the water heater, and the curtain falls as he wraps the tube around his hand and carries it off.

As with *All My Sons*, the first act of *Death of a Salesman* ends on an edgy, mysterious note. Linda's question to Willy about Biff's resentment hints at a long-kept secret, this one between father and son. Just as Ann's homecoming leads to an upheaval in *All My Sons*, Biff's return at this crucial moment in Willy's life signals change.

ACT TWO—THE RECKONING

Act two begins the following morning, on a seemingly sunny note. Biff and Happy have already left for the city, and optimistic, Willy promises Linda that he is going to ask Howard for a transfer and an advance to make the final payment on their house.

As soon as Willy sits down in his young boss's office, however, Howard forces Willy to listen to a recording he made of his family on his new wire recording machine. After listening politely to the silly recording, Willy asks Howard about working in New York. Unsympathetic, Howard informs

Willy that he has no spot for him in New York, despite earlier statements to the contrary.

Growing desperate, Willy tells Howard about Dave Singleman, a salesman he met when he was nineteen, at the point in his life when he was deciding whether to go on selling or search with Ben for his wayward father in Alaska. Willy was so impressed by Dave, who at age eighty-four was still selling successfully on the road, that he decided to remain a salesman himself. "Do you know? when he died—and by the way he died the death of a salesman, in his green velvet slippers in the smoker of the New York, New Haven and Hartford, going into Boston—when he died, hundreds of salesmen and buyers were at his funeral."[11] When Dave was alive, Willy notes, salesmen were treated with more respect.

Unimpressed by the tale, Howard tries to convince Willy to leave his office. Willy refuses to be dismissed, however, and declares that years before, when Howard's father ran the business, "there were promises made across this desk."[12] Willy confesses that after giving thirty-four years to the company, he does not have enough money to pay his life insurance premium and begs for a salary. Fed up, Howard reminds Willy that he was never a great seller, and Willy begins to shout at him. Finally, after Howard tells Willy that he should go to his sons for help, Willy understands that he is being fired.

In a daze Willy fades into a memory of his brother Ben's final visit: As he is leaving the Lomans', Ben offers Willy a job overseeing his company in Alaska. Linda discourages Willy from accepting, and convinced that Howard's father is going to make him a member of the firm, Willy turns Ben down. The Lomans and Bernard then take off for Ebbets Field, where Biff is playing in the championship high school football game.

Coming out of his reverie, Willy finds himself in Charley's office and runs into Bernard. When Bernard, now a successful lawyer, asks how Biff and Happy are doing, Willy at first brags about Biff's lucrative business deals. He then admits that Biff has been squandering his life since high school and asks Bernard for advice.

In response, Bernard asks Willy why Biff, who flunked the math exam, never took the class over in summer school so he could go to college. Willy responds by saying, "Bernard, that question has been trailing me like a ghost for the last fifteen years."[13] Bernard reveals that after Biff returned from seeing Willy in Boston following the test, he found him crying in the cellar. When Bernard asks Willy what happened to Biff in Boston, Willy becomes defensive and refuses to answer. Charley then calls Willy into his office, and Willy asks his neighbor for 110 dollars, enough money to pay his life insurance premium. Charley, who has been lending Willy money every week since he went off salary, gives Willy the money but again suggests that he take a job with him. Again Willy refuses, and Charley accuses him of being jealous and prideful. After observing that he is worth more "dead than alive," Willy leaves, despondent.

The action shifts to a restaurant, where Biff and Happy have arranged to meet Willy for dinner. Happy has arrived first and flirts with Miss Forsythe, a lavishly made-up woman at the next table. When Biff walks in, Happy tries to interest him in the woman, but Biff is distracted and confesses he did a "terrible thing" that day.

Biff admits that after he waited outside Oliver's office for six hours, Oliver finally called him in, but did not remember him. Biff had introduced himself to Oliver as his former salesman, but after Oliver gave him a "look," Biff suddenly remembered he had only been a shipping clerk. "I realized what a ridiculous lie my whole life has been! We've been talking in a dream for fifteen years."[14] Biff then divulges that after Oliver left him alone in his office, he stole his fountain pen and ran out of the building.

Just then Willy arrives, and Biff tries to tell him the bad news. Willy interrupts, however, and reveals he has been fired. Seeing his father's distress, Biff starts to lie about his meeting with Oliver, pretending all went well. When Willy jumps in and adds his own lies and distortions, however, Biff cannot go on and returns to the truth.

As Biff describes his meeting with Oliver and the theft of the pen, Willy's mind shifts to the past, to the day when Biff found out he had flunked his math exam and decided to take the train to Boston. In Willy's mind Biff's confession about Oliver becomes intertwined with his painful memory about Boston, the secret he and Biff have been keeping.

Willy grows increasingly agitated, and when Miss Forsythe reappears with a girlfriend, he rushes into the men's room. Unable to cope, Biff, who also admits he once stole basketballs from Oliver's store, storms out of the restaurant. Happy tells the women that Willy is "just a guy," and the three leave to follow Biff, abandoning Willy in the bathroom.

The scene playing out in Willy's head, meanwhile, concludes: In the Boston hotel room, Willy is with The Woman when persistent knocking is heard at the door. After hiding The Woman in the bathroom, Willy finally opens the door to find Biff. Distraught, Biff tells Willy about flunking his math class, and Willy promises to return home and fix things with the teacher. Before he can get Biff out of the room, however, The Woman emerges from the bathroom, laughing.

After demanding the stockings Willy had promised her, The Woman finally exits. Despite Willy's denials, Biff deduces that Willy has been cheating on his mother and starts to cry. Through his tears Biff calls Willy a "fake," then leaves. Back in the present Willy realizes he has been abandoned by his sons and stumbles out of the restaurant after asking the waiter where he can buy seeds to plant.

Later that night Biff and Happy return home and are met by a furious Linda. Linda berates her sons for cruelly walking out on Willy in the restaurant and calls the drunken Biff a "louse."

Willy, meanwhile, is in the backyard with a flashlight, trying to plant carrot seeds in the dark. Imagining Ben is with him, Willy talks about committing suicide so that Linda can collect the twenty-thousand-dollar life insurance benefit. Ben calls Willy's plan risky and cowardly, but Willy compares it to a "diamond, shining in the dark, hard and rough, that I can pick up and touch in my hand. Not like—like an appointment!"[15]

Biff interrupts Willy's imaginings and announces he is leaving for good. Although Biff is willing to accept the blame for what went wrong between them, Willy continues to accuse Biff of spiting him. Fed up, Biff lays Willy's suicide pipe on the table and reveals that he spent three months in a Kansas City jail for theft. "I stole myself out of every good job since high school! . . . And I never got anywhere because you blew me so full of hot air I could never stand taking orders from anybody!"[16]

Exhausted by his outburst, Biff finally collapses in tears in Willy's arms. Suddenly realizing that Biff loves him and always has, Willy resolves to carry out his plan to give Biff seed money to start a business. After the others have gone to bed, Willy, still replaying his past, slips into his car and speeds off. Seconds later, Linda, Biff, and Happy are jolted by the sound of a horrible crash.

Act two ends as Linda, Happy, Biff, Bernard, and Charley approach Willy's fresh grave. The requiem continues at the graveside, where five mourners talk about Willy and his life as a salesman. Although Happy and Charley defend Willy's choices, Biff insists that his father never knew who he really was. Linda can only cry for her lost companion. "I made the last payment on the house today," she tells Willy, sobbing. "Today, dear. And there'll be nobody home. . . . We're free and clear. . . . We're free."[17]

THEMES AND CHARACTERS

Willy Loman, Inside and Out

> How may a man make of the outside world a home? How and in what ways must he struggle, what must he strive to change and overcome within himself and outside himself if he is to find the safety, the surrounding of love, the ease of soul, the sense of identity and honor which, evidently, all men have connected in their memories with the idea of family?[18]

According to Miller, these are the primary questions posed by *Death of a Salesman*.

With *Death of a Salesman*, Miller explores many of the same themes and character types examined in *All My Sons*. Like the earlier play, *Death of a Salesman* works on both a personal or psychological level and on a social level. As with Joe Keller, Willy's problems—his guilt, regret, and confusion—are the result of his own personal shortcomings as well as society's. Willy is a more complex character than Keller, however, and his family is in some ways more deeply troubled than the Kellers.

Throughout the play Willy struggles to make a home of the outside world. As a young man, Willy is asked to choose between his get-rich-quick brother,

Ben (and by extension their wayward father), and elderly Dave Singleman. Willy chooses Dave, the supersalesman, who becomes Willy's father substitute and mentor. Years later Ben, now a wealthy businessman, returns to the Lomans' and again asks Willy to join him. Although by this time Willy is discontented and confused, he tells Ben that he must stay in Brooklyn for his sons' sake. As an old man, Willy is haunted by the memory of Ben and the lost opportunities he seems to represent, but still cannot break free of Dave's salesman dream.

In the play's first extended memory scene Miller presents all of the plot and character points that will become crucial to the development of the play: Willy's insecurities about work; his dishonest, contradictory relationships with his family; and his overemphasis on winning and competing. By connecting The Woman to Linda's pep talk and her stocking-mending, Miller also suggests Willy's guilt about the affair.

In the end Willy accepts that he is a failure but fails to understand why. Despite years of evidence to the contrary, he fights the notion that he has always been a poor salesman with corrupt dreams. Biff is convinced that Willy, a gifted carpenter, would have been happier working with his hands, but Willy insists that such physical labor is beneath him.

Willy goes to his death declaring that as a salesman, he is well known and well liked, just like Dave Singleman. As Miller shows, however, Willy is not liked, and, in contrast to Dave, has only five mourners at his funeral. Willy also dies believing that his sons will use the insurance money, not to find their own place in the world, but to follow in his deluded footsteps. In other words, Willy fails to make the outside world a home because he has always presented a "fake" front to the outside world.

Biff and Happy

Willy also fails in his relationships at home, especially in his relationship with Biff, his favorite son. When Biff discovers his father's affair, he breaks down, then withdraws from Willy and his dreams. Having once revered his father, Biff now rejects him, not only because he is loyal to his mother but also because he has seen the falseness of Willy's life. For Biff, Willy's private lies, adulteries, and exaggerations are the same as his phony salesman's pitch. He loves his father, but cannot follow or applaud him.

Because of Willy's misguided dreams, both Biff and Happy have been unable to mature and move on. Biff drifts from place to place, stealing himself out of jobs, while Happy strays from woman to woman, lying himself out of lasting relationships. Happy, the

LIFE AND DEATH OF THE SALESMAN

less-loved second child, strives to get his father's attention but never succeeds, while Biff receives excessive, inappropriate attention from Willy.

The following exchange, which takes place when Biff and Happy are teenagers, demonstrates the dynamics in Willy's relationship with his sons. In the scene Happy runs in with a surprise gift, a punching bag, that Willy has brought home for Biff:

> BIFF: Gee, how'd you know we wanted a punching bag?
> WILLY: Well, it's the finest thing for the timing.
> HAPPY, *lies down on his back and pedals with his feet:* I'm losing weight, you notice, Pop?
> WILLY, *to Happy*: Jumping rope is good too.
> BIFF: Did you see the new football I got?
> WILLY, *examining the ball:* Where'd you get a new ball?
> BIFF: The coach told me to practice my passing.
> WILLY: That so? And he gave you the ball, heh?
> BIFF: Well, I borrowed it from the locker room. *He laughs confidentially.*
> WILLY, *laughing with him at the theft:* I want you to return that.
> HAPPY: I told you he wouldn't like it!
> BIFF, *angrily:* Well, I'm bringing it back!
> WILLY, *stopping the incipient argument, to Happy:* Sure, he's gotta practice with a regulation ball, doesn't he? *To Biff:* Coach'll probably congratulate you on your initiative![19]

In just a few lines Miller dramatizes Willy's favoritism toward Biff. After being ordered to fetch Biff's punching bag from Willy's car, Happy tries to impress his father with his exercising, but is all but ignored. Willy has brought nothing for Happy and makes it clear that the punching bag is Biff's alone. When Happy says to Biff about the stolen football, "I told you he wouldn't like it!" Willy comes to Biff's defense and ends up foolishly condoning the theft.

All that is rotten in Willy's relationship with his sons is laid out in this act one scene. Instead of teaching his children honesty, kindness, and fairness, he encourages them to be competitive with each other and to ignore the consequences of their actions. By contrast, neighbor Charlie's son, Bernard, while not athletic or popular, is hardworking and loyal. Thanks to Charlie, Bernard grows up to be a highly successful, well-adjusted lawyer. When the adult Biff finally reveals he is a petty thief and Happy admits he is a liar, the heartbreaking results of Willy's parenting are fully illuminated.

Linda

Like Kate in *All My Sons*, Linda Loman is a determined wife and mother. In many ways Miller portrays her as a typical married woman of the period—a housewife whose identity is tied to her husband's. Although she knows that Willy is not the salesman he claims to be, and that his plans for Biff and Happy are unlikely to materialize, she never confronts him directly with the truth. Instead, she tries to lead him gently back to reality, just as she tries to lead him gently inside the house or to bed. She knows what Willy is and where he is headed, but like Kate in *All My Sons*, she fights for his survival as though for her own.

Linda's support of Willy is crucial to the play because without it, Willy would be a pathetic individual, unworthy of the reader's concern. She is in effect the spokesperson for Willy's good side. More than any other character in the play, Linda defends Willy's humanity and his right to be treated with decency and respect. Her cry that "attention must be paid" to her dying salesman husband is both a personal cry for kindness and a public cry for justice.

THE LOMANS AND THE AMERICAN DREAM

Like Keller and Chris in *All My Sons*, Willy and Biff are products of their social class and milieu. Like Keller, Willy believes in the American dream, while Biff, like

Chris, is skeptical of it. The key difference between the Kellers and the Lomans, however, is that the Kellers have achieved the American dream, while the Lomans are still chasing it.

Having lived through the deprivation of the Depression, Miller empathizes with the Lomans' financial problems. As dramatic scholar Brian Parker observed about the play: "Miller documents a world of arch-supports, aspirin, spectacles, subways, time payments, advertising, Chevrolets, faulty refrigerators, life insurance, mortgages. . . ."[20] Miller makes Linda's down-to-the-penny budgeting, her determination to make the final payment on the house so that she and Willy can be "free and clear," not only sympathetic but almost heroic in its sincerity.

After it opened, some critics described *Death of a Salesman* as a condemnation of postwar capitalism. In their minds the working-class Lomans were victims of America's heartless pursuit of wealth. Willy slaves for the "almighty dollar," then after thirty-four years on the job is tossed out with nothing. Unlike Keller in *All My Sons*, who produces hard goods, Willy's financial success is dependent on the fickle world of buyers and sellers. Miller makes it clear, however, that Willy's plight, like his Uncle Manny's, is as much his own fault as the system's.

WILLY LOMAN, TRAGIC HERO?

Since its opening, critics have argued about whether *Death of a Salesman* can be considered a tragedy. In classical tragedies, which derive from ancient Greek drama, the tragic hero is always a person of high birth and importance. He has a superior character overall but is plagued by a fatal flaw—jealousy, greed, ambition, and so on. In the course of the drama, the hero's moral fiber is tested, and his fatal flaw causes him to make an immoral or unwise choice. His choice leads not only to his own downfall but wreaks havoc on others. To be classically tragic, the hero must recognize his part in what has happened and feel great remorse. Often his remorse leads to self-destruction.

Is *Death of a Salesman* a tragedy? In his review of the play, critic William Hawkins wrote: *"Death of a Salesman* is a play written along the lines of the finest classical tragedy. It is the revelation of a man's downfall, in destruction whose roots are entirely in his own soul. The play builds to an immutable conflict where there is no resolution for this man in his life."[21] John Mason Brown, on the other hand, wrote in his review: "Mr. Miller's play is a tragedy modern and personal, not classic and heroic. Its central figure is a little man sentenced to discover his smallness rather than a big man undone by his greatness."[22]

Both descriptions of the play are accurate, although Hawkins's phrase "classical tragedy" is misleading. Willy Loman is not a tragic hero in the Greek tradition. Obviously, he is not a man of high birth. Nor is he particularly virtuous, nor does he possess a single fatal flaw. He is a bundle of good and bad, the victim of both his own shortcomings—pride, envy, dishonesty—and circumstance. When *Death of a Salesman* opened in New York, Miller defended the play as tragedy, writing in an essay "that the common man is as apt a subject for tragedy in its highest sense as kings were."[23] Willy is tragic in that his shortcomings cause great pain for himself and his family, and at the end of the story, he sacrifices himself through suicide.

In his introduction to his collected plays, Miller wrote about Willy in act two:

> In terms of his character, he has achieved a very powerful piece of knowledge, which is that he is loved by his son and has been embraced by him and forgiven. . . . That he is unable to take this victory thoroughly to his heart, that it closes the circle for him and propels him to his death, is the wage of his sin. . . ."[24]

70

As the play's title suggests, *Death of a Salesman* is the story of one salesman, Willy Loman. But it is also the story of the American salesman.

In his 1958 essay "Morality and Modern Drama," Miller wrote: "A salesman is a kind of creative person. . . . They have to get up in the morning and conceive a plan of attack and use all kinds of ingenuity all day long just like a writer does. . . . He believes that selling is the greatest thing anybody can do."[25]

Willy Loman, Miller's protagonist in *Death of a Salesman*, is a drummer—a salesman who represents a company on the road. He does not sell his company's products directly to the customer, door-to-door, but to stores and distributors. Drummers try to convince buyers to place bulk orders for their company's products. Armed with product samples, they travel from city to city, usually within a single region. Willy, for example, is his company's "New England man."

When Willy tells his boss, Howard, about Dave Singleman, the elderly salesman who inspired Willy to stick with drumming, he is remembering the early 1900s. Personalized selling was at its peak during that time, and salesmen enjoyed a good reputation with the public. The Depression, however, changed not only people's buying habits but their perception of salesmen as well. Because very few people had money to spend, salesmen were regarded with suspicion and contempt.

After World War II, when *Death of a Salesman* is set, the American salesman endured another change. Following many years of war rationing, the American market was flooded with goods, especially cars and appliances, and people were eager to buy. Mass marketing, advertising directly to the public, had become standard practice, and the need for the kind of face-to-face drumming that Willy practiced decreased.

As Willy says to Howard in describing Dave Singleman, "In those days there was personality in it, Howard. There was respect, and comradeship, and gratitude in it. Today, it's all cut and dried, and there's no chance for bringing friendship to bear—or personality."[26]

THEATRICAL STYLE

Stylistically, *Death of a Salesman* is a complicated piece, much more so than *All My Sons*. Although both plays deal with the past, only *Death of a Salesman* brings the past to life. *Death of a Salesman* is also unique in that most of the narrative is told strongly through one character's point of view—Willy's.

How does Miller guide his audience between the different time periods and places of Willy's mind?

One stage device Miller uses to distinguish time and place is lighting. As the first memory scene in act one begins, for example, Miller notes in the stage directions:

> . . . Willy's form is dimly seen below in the darkened kitchen. He opens the refrigerator, searches in there, and takes out a bottle of milk. The apartment houses are fading out, and the entire house and surroundings become covered with leaves.[27]

The light then rises on the kitchen, and Willy, who has been mumbling to an invisible Biff, shuts the refrigerator. The scene shifts completely into the past, to a late autumn afternoon during Biff and Happy's high-school days. By lowering and raising the light levels, Miller signals to the audience that the time frame is changing.

A similar transformation takes place in the scene

in which The Woman is introduced. In the stage directions Miller indicates that at first The Woman can only be "dimly seen" dressing behind a scrim—a semitransparent cloth curtain—on the side of the stage. As the scene begins in earnest the lights brighten, and The Woman comes from behind the scrim and into full view.

The movement of the actors on the set are another way that Miller helps the audience with time shifts. In the opening stage directions Miller advises:

> Whenever the action is in the present the actors observe the imaginary wall-lines, entering the house only through its door at the left. But in the scenes of the past these boundaries are broken, and characters enter or leave a room by stepping "through" a wall onto the forestage.[28]

The stage directions also instruct the actors to speak in ways that illuminate the time shifts. As the first extended memory scene begins, for example, Miller notes that Willy is to speak to a point offstage, not mumbling as before, but talking at normal conversational volume.

In addition to lighting and movement, Miller creates sound motifs to underscore some of the characters. Willy, for one, has his own "theme" music, which is played on a solo flute, the instrument his long-lost father once made and played. The flute theme accompanies Willy in the present and is heard at the end of the play as Linda speaks over Willy's grave. Ben also has his own recognizable theme music, while raucous laughter always signals the arrival of The Woman.

LANGUAGE

More so than in *All My Sons*, speech in *Death of a Salesman* is stylized. Miller gives each of his characters distinctive conversational quirks. Contradictions, for example, characterize Willy's speech. At the start of act one, Willy describes Biff first as "a lazy bum," then a few lines later says, "There's one thing about Biff—he's not lazy."[29] Willy gushes about his old Chevrolet, then curses the brand, whining, "they ought to prohibit the manufacture of that car!"[30] He calls himself well liked, then in the next breath complains that he is not well liked.

Happy—the vain, insecure womanizer—is always asking, "Aren't I losing weight?" and declaring that he is "going to get married" despite having no girlfriend. By contrast, Biff's speech is filled with references to nature and building things. In his scenes Ben gushes about African jungles and diamonds, images that correspond to his adventurousness and wealth. In addition to laughing, The

Woman repeatedly tells Willy, "I'll put you right through to the buyers." All of these verbal quirks and repetitions help define the characters and function as verbal shorthand for the audience. They are the word equivalents of Miller's musical motifs.

CRUCIBLES

Examining *The Crucible*

After his *Death of a Salesman* triumph Miller went back and forth between three projects. While struggling with what he described as his "third" play, he wrote an English language version of Henrik Ibsen's 1882 *An Enemy of the People* and teamed up with Elia Kazan on *The Hook*, a screenplay inspired by his days on the New York docks.

An Enemy of the People, a social drama about a doctor who fights to have his town's new health spa shut down after he discovers that the water feeding it is dangerously polluted, opened in New York in December 1950. Miller updated Ibsen's dialogue for American audiences and trimmed the original's five acts to three. Although it was well received by critics, Miller's adaptation has puzzled modern-day scholars, who view it as an odd hybrid of two masters.

Miller's collaboration on *The Hook*, which chronicled corruption in the waterfront unions, was even less successful. Despite Kazan's good standing in Hollywood, the story was labeled "communistic" at a time when America was very sensitive to such politics, and the film was never made. *The Hook* proved to be only the first of many confrontations Miller would have with anticommunist forces during the 1950s.

HUAC—THE TWENTIETH-CENTURY WITCH HUNT

Like many artists and intellectuals of his generation, Arthur Miller became involved in socialist politics during the Depression. He believed that socialism and its sister movement, communism, had much to offer the poor and underprivileged in America. In the late 1940s, after aggressive acts by the Soviet Union (now Russia) in postwar Europe, America's leaders became obsessed with stopping communism, the Soviet Union's only political party. Because no actual battles were fought by the two countries, America's struggle with the Soviet Union was dubbed the "cold war."

In the U.S. Congress a committee of conservative leaders led by Senator Joseph McCarthy began publicly identifying Americans whom they suspected of being communists and "communist sympathizers," forcing them to testify at hearings about their political affiliations. The committee, called the House on Un-American Activities Committee (HUAC), also demanded that those called to testify identify colleagues and friends who had participated in communist activities.

Although membership in the Communist Party was legal in the United States, HUAC had the authority to convict witnesses who refused to "name names" of contempt of Congress and to send them to jail. Initially, HUAC focused its attention on Hollywood. The first group of actors, directors, and writers to be tried by HUAC became known as the Hollywood Ten. Like others who followed, the Hollywood Ten were blacklisted, or banned, from working in the entertainment industry. Many screen artists' careers, and in some cases lives, were destroyed by HUAC. Eventually the anticommunist furor spread beyond Hollywood. Ordinary citizens, some of whom had no communist connections whatsoever, became caught in its net.

In 1952, to voice his outrage against the increasingly powerful HUAC, Miller began writing *The Crucible*, a play about the infamous Salem witch trials of 1692. Miller saw disturbing similarities between McCarthy's hunt for communists and Colonial America's hunt for witches, and hoped that a drama about the country's past might shed light on its present.

He also saw similarities between Kazan, who in April 1952 had named names before HUAC, and many of the so-called witches who "confessed" in

Arthur Miller waits at the witness table shortly before testifying before the House on Un-American Activities Committee (HUAC) in Washington, D.C., on June 21, 1956.

Salem. Kazan's submission to HUAC saved his movie career, but he lost many friends and the respect of his peers. Although Miller eventually forgave Kazan, their partnership was forever damaged.

Less obviously than Kazan's and HUAC's influence on *The Crucible* were Miller's troubled marriage to Mary and his growing physical attraction to movie star Marilyn Monroe. He met Monroe in Hollywood while promoting the screenplay of *The Hook* and

79

observing film production on *Death of a Salesman*. Although Miller dedicated *The Crucible* to Mary, it was the last full-length play he would write while married to her.

Directed by Jed Harris, *The Crucible* opened on January 22, 1953, at the Martin Beck Theatre. It received mixed reviews—some critics called it cold and little more than a political pamphlet—and closed after 197 performances. Despite its dubious beginnings, *The Crucible* won a Tony Award and went on to become Miller's most-produced play. It was born in response to a specific political event but is regarded today as a timeless parable about the corruption of power.

PLOT AND STRUCTURE

In narrative structure *The Crucible* resembles *Death of a Salesman* more than *All My Sons*. Although it contains four acts instead of two, the first two acts relate to each other, as do the last two acts. The first two and the last two parts are connected by place and action. Acts one and two take place in homes, while acts three and four are set in public places. In the first two acts the "crime" is identified and the "criminals" are arrested. In the final acts the accused are tried and punished.

Unlike *All My Sons* and *Death of a Salesman*, *The Crucible* contains very little backstory. Except for one secret, which is revealed halfway through the play, the past does not play an important role in the drama. The play begins almost in mid-action.

Perhaps because of the play's historical origins, Miller does not present the drama strongly from one point of view. He does not try to get inside his protagonist's head, as he did in *Death of a Salesman*. Instead, recognizing the inherent power of the real story, Miller allows the narrative to reveal itself on its own terms.

In a 1958 revised, published version of the play, Miller sprinkled historical notes, or asides, about the characters throughout the text. As originally conceived, these asides were to be narrated by an onstage "reader." Although some published versions of the play include the asides, they are rarely performed. Their inclusion in the written text, however, provides the reader with additional information about Miller's dramatic intentions.

ACT ONE—OVERTURE

Act one of *The Crucible*, which Miller subtitles "An Overture," immediately plunges the reader into the story's conflict. The curtain rises on a small upstairs bedroom in the home of Reverend Parris of Salem, Massachusetts. Parris is praying over his ten-year-old daughter, Betty, who is lying "inert" on her bed. When his servant, Tituba, asks how Betty is doing, Parris breaks down in sobs. His "strikingly beautiful" seventeen-year-old niece, Abigail, an orphan, then enters with another girl, Susanna Walcott.

Sent there by the town physician, Susanna reveals the doctor's suspicions that Betty, whom Parris discovered dancing "like a heathen" with Abigail in the forest, is the victim of witchcraft. Declaring that he has many "enemies" who would use Betty's illness as an excuse to drive him from his ministry, Parris demands that Abigail tell him what she, Betty, and other girls were doing with Tituba in the forest.

Abigail swears that she and the others were merely dancing to Tituba's Barbados songs and hotly denies that her former employer, Elizabeth Proctor, threw her out of her house for scandalous reasons. Abigail, who was the Proctors' servant, insists that the "cold" Goody Proctor fired her because Abigail refused to be her "slave."

Villagers Ann and Thomas Putnam then enter and declare that their daughter, Ruth, is walking around like a zombie and that some villagers claim to have seen Betty "flying" the night before. Ann also reveals that Tituba was trying to contact the spirits of Ann's seven dead infants, each of whom died in childbirth, when Parris came upon them in the forest. Parris is upset to learn that Ann has been "conjuring spirits," a sin, but agrees to lead the crowd gathering downstairs in a hymn.

Once alone with Betty, Mercy Lewis, the Putnams' servant, and Mary Warren, the Proctors' servant, Abigail issues a warning to keep silent. Betty, hysterical, bolts up and reminds Abigail that she "drank blood" as part of a curse against Elizabeth Proctor. Abigail smacks Betty and orders them all to admit only to dancing and conjuring Ann's dead children.

A few moments later farmer John Proctor, Elizabeth's husband, enters the bedroom. Intimidated, Mercy and Mary scurry away, leaving Proctor alone with Abigail. While dismissing the witchcraft rumors, Abigail flirts with Proctor, hinting at a prior sexual relationship, but he rebuffs her. Over his protests, Abigail insists that Proctor still desires her and pledges her love.

Just then, in reaction to the word "Jesus" in Reverend Parris's downstairs hymn, Betty starts wailing. Betty's violent reaction to hearing the Lord's name further convinces the Putnams that the girl is possessed by the Devil. Parris then argues with Putnam about his work contract, which Putnam oversees, and with Proctor about his poor church attendance.

The discussion among the men heats up until Reverend John Hale of nearby Beverly walks in. After inspecting the now speechless Betty, Hale questions Abigail and Tituba about the previous night. Abigail claims that Tituba forced her to drink blood, and Hale accuses Tituba of witchcraft. To save herself, Tituba admits "compacting" with the Devil and, at Hale's urging, identifies midwife Goody Osburn and Sarah Good as her accomplices.

In a frenzy, Abigail then confesses that she, too, "wrote in the Devil's book" and names Bridget Bishop as a third conspirator. Betty suddenly stirs and, along with Abigail, begins shouting out names of other Devil worshippers. Act one ends on the girls' "ecstatic cries."

ACT TWO—ACCUSATION

Act two begins eight days later, in the Proctors' modest farmhouse. Elizabeth informs Proctor that their servant, Mary Warren, is an "official" in the General Court in Salem, where the women accused of witchcraft are being tried. When Proctor, who has confessed his infidelity to the sickly Elizabeth, reveals that he was briefly alone with Abigail at the Parrises', Elizabeth grows cold and demands that Proctor go to Boston and expose the teenager's lies.

Pale and weak, Mary returns from Boston and announces that thirty-nine women now stand accused of witchcraft. After giving Elizabeth a rag doll she made while in court, Mary reveals that due to her testimony, Goody Osburn, a beggar, has been sentenced to hang. Though upset, Mary defends her actions, noting that Goody Osburn could save herself by "confessing." Mary then states that Elizabeth was accused, but refuses to say by whom.

Elizabeth declares to Proctor that Abigail must be her accuser and "wants her dead." Although Proctor vows to straighten matters out with the court, Elizabeth suspects he is still attracted to Abigail and will not publicly attack her. Proctor protests, saying "your spirit twists around the single error of my life."[1]

Just then, Reverend Hale, an expert in "demonic arts," arrives at the house. After confirming that Elizabeth and the saintly Rebecca Nurse have been mentioned in court, Hale questions Proctor about his spotty church attendance. While defending his piety, Proctor admits that he does not like the greedy, shallow Parris. After Hale cautions Proctor about judging Parris, Elizabeth compels her husband to expose Abigail's lie. Though reluctant, Proctor agrees to testify in court that according to Abigail, the girls faked their afflictions to avoid punishment for dancing.

Before Hale leaves, however, elderly Giles Corey and Francis Nurse burst in to announce that Giles's wife, Martha, has been charged with witchcraft.

Giles is particularly distressed because he knows that he brought suspicion upon Martha when he asked if her book-reading might be a sign of bewitchment. After Giles points out that Martha's accuser recently had a financial dispute with her, tailor Ezekiel Cheever arrives with an arrest warrant for Elizabeth.

Cheever reveals that Abigail has accused Elizabeth and offers the rag doll, into which a pin has been stuck, as proof of Elizabeth's sorcery. Cheever states that earlier that evening Abigail collapsed in pain and was found with a pin jabbed in her belly, the obvious victim of malicious sorcery. Mary admits that Abigail may have put the pin in the doll herself but refuses to accuse her publicly.

Enraged, Proctor rips up Cheever's warrant, proclaiming that "crazy children are jangling the keys of the kingdom and common vengeance writes the law!"[2] Elizabeth is, nonetheless, arrested and taken away in chains, and Proctor confronts Mary in a fury. When Mary informs Proctor that if crossed, Abigail will expose his infidelity, Proctor states that then "we will slide together into our pit."[3] Act two concludes as Proctor demands that the terrified Mary confess the truth, noting that "we are only what we always were, but naked now."[4]

ACT THREE—CONFESSION

Act three takes place in the vestry outside the Salem meetinghouse, which is now serving as a courtroom for the witch trials. As the real trial proceeds next door, an unofficial trial begins to unfold in the "solemn" outer room.

Having been ejected from his wife's trial, Giles Corey confronts Deputy Governor Danforth, Judge Hathorne, Hale, and Parris, but they are unmoved by his pleas. Proctor then enters with Mary, who, at Proctor's urging, finally confesses that the girls have been lying and faking. Danforth is skeptical of Mary's about-face, however, and begins to drill Proctor. Proctor defends his piety, but Cheever informs the governor that Proctor sometimes plows his fields on Sunday instead of attending church, a significant breach of Christian practice.

Proctor then learns from Danforth that the imprisoned Elizabeth now claims to be pregnant. Again Danforth is suspicious, but Proctor insists his wife is incapable of lying. Danforth pledges to postpone Elizabeth's trial for a month and if at that time she is visibly pregnant to delay her trial for another year. Dissatisfied with Danforth's meager concession, Proctor shows him the signatures of ninety-one villagers who have testified to the good character of Elizabeth, Rebecca, and Martha. Parris immediately denounces the document, and Danforth orders that all ninety-one signers be brought in for questioning.

Giles charges Putnam with encouraging his daughter to accuse a neighbor of witchcraft so that Putnam can buy the neighbor's land. Giles, however, will not reveal the name of the person who overheard Putnam. After Danforth orders that Giles be arrested for contempt of court, Proctor presents a signed statement from Mary, who swears that the girls have been faking their bewitchment.

Danforth brings Abigail, Mercy, and others in to face Mary. Abigail accuses Mary of lying, and Danforth insists that Mary pretend to faint and turn cold, as she says she did in court. When Mary is unable to faint on command, an angry Danforth begins to question Abigail. Suddenly Abigail claims to feel a cold wind blowing and starts to shiver.

The other girls join in, and infuriated, Proctor grabs Abigail by the hair and calls her a "whore." Proctor then confesses his adultery and tells a shocked Danforth that Abigail "thinks to dance with me on my wife's grave."[5] To test Proctor's story, Danforth orders Elizabeth be brought in, but she refuses to accuse Proctor of sleeping with Abigail. As Elizabeth is led out of the vestry, Proctor cries out to Danforth that she is lying to protect him. Hale, whose convictions have been wavering, agrees with Proctor and admits he no longer believes Abigail's stories.

Before Danforth can react to Hale, Abigail screams at the ceiling and, claiming to see something there, shrieks in terror. The other girls follow suit, pointing wildly at the ceiling and yelling, and Abigail claims that Mary's spirit has become a huge, evil bird. When Mary protests, Abigail and the girls begin copying her as though possessed. Although Proctor and Hale denounce Abigail's stunt, Mary, fearing she will be implicated as a witch, turns on Proctor and says he is in league with the Devil and forced her to lie.

Condemned by Danforth, Proctor warns that he and Danforth are both frauds and will "burn together" in hell. After Proctor and Giles are hauled off to prison, Hale quits the court in disgust, and Act three ends.

ACT FOUR—REDEMPTION

Act four opens the following autumn, in a prison cell holding Sarah Good and Tituba, who is now half-mad. Both women have confessed to being witches, and after they are moved to another cell, Danforth, Hathorne, and Parris enter the cell to discuss that day's scheduled executions. Although Danforth is pleased to hear that Hale is trying to persuade Elizabeth and Rebecca Nurse to confess, Parris reveals that in nearby Andover the townspeople are rebelling against the courts in their own witchcraft case. Parris then admits that Abigail stole his savings and fled the village, and that his life is being threatened. Parris warns that unlike the twelve people who have already been hanged, the villagers who are to be executed that morning are respectable and well liked.

After announcing that Rebecca has refused to confess, Hale begs Danforth to postpone the executions. Hale tells the governor that because of the hangings, Salem has become a village of orphans and abandoned farms. The ambitious Danforth, however, insists on carrying out the sentences.

To alleviate his guilt, Hale then convinces the pregnant but still imprisoned Elizabeth to speak to Proctor, who is condemned to die that morning. Proctor is brought up from the dungeon, where he has been languishing alone in chains. Elizabeth tells Proctor about Rebecca's courageous denials and says that Giles refused to admit or deny his guilt even as heavy stones were being piled on his chest. He died defiant, she says, commanding his torturers to put on "more weight."

After Proctor admits he is thinking about confessing, feeling he is unworthy of dying with the others, he asks Elizabeth for forgiveness. Instead, Elizabeth apologizes for being a cold, suspicious wife and tells Proctor that she can neither encourage nor condemn him for confessing. In Danforth's presence Proctor lies that he did the "Devil's work" but repeatedly refuses to implicate Rebecca as a witch. Reluctantly Danforth lets the matter drop and demands that Proctor sign his confession. Proctor signs, then—realizing that Danforth intends to use the document to justify his corrupt cause—snatches the paper back and tears it up.

Danforth orders Proctor, Rebecca, and the others to hang "high over the town," and Proctor is led out. Though heartbroken, Elizabeth refuses to plead with Proctor to save himself, saying, "He have his goodness now. God forbid I take it from him!"[6] As the morning's sunlight fills the cell Proctor bravely goes to his death.

SALEM WITCH TRIALS— HISTORY AS DRAMA

Although *All My Sons* was inspired by an actual legal case, *The Crucible* marked Miller's first attempt at dramatizing a historical event. Miller first became interested in the Salem witch trials after reading Marion Starkey's book *The Devil in Massachusetts*. Miller then spent ten days in Salem reading official

Period Vocabulary

The following are words and phrases from *The Crucible* and their less familiar seventeenth-century definitions.

blink—To ignore (*I cannot blink what I saw*)

bring to book—To call to justice, make accountable (*I have been too quick to bring the man to book*)

familiar spirit—A supernatural spirit or demon that serves a person (*Your wife's familiar spirit pushed it in*)

goody—A polite form of address for a woman of nonaristocratic social standing (*Goody Putnam*)

gull—To deceive, trick (*They're gulling you, mister*)

marvelous—Improbable, incredible (*It is a marvelous sign*)

misty—Obscure, unclear (*There is a misty plot afoot*)

quail—To lose heart or courage (*We dare not quail to follow*)

rebel—To cause to reject, repel (*It rebels my stomach*)

sport—To treat lightly, or to tease (*Do you sport with me?*)

text—Theme, subject (*Has the court discovered a text in poppets now?*)

white—Decent, honorable, of good reputation (*Your name in the town—it is entirely white, is it not?*)

records of the trials at the courthouse and the local historical society.

In an opening note to the play, Miller advises:

This play is not history in the sense in which the word is used by the academic historian. Dramatic purposes have sometimes required many characters to be fused into one: the number of girls involved in the "crying out" has been reduced;

Abigail's age has been raised; while there were several judges of almost equal authority, I have symbolized them all in Hathorne and Danforth. However, I believe that the reader will discover here the essential nature of one of the strangest and most awful chapters in human history. The fate of each character is exactly that of his historical model, and there is no one in the drama who did not play a similar—and is some cases exactly the same—role in history.[7]

As Miller points out, some of the play's action was invented, most notably John Proctor's public admission of adultery. Although Abigail Williams had been a servant in the Proctor home and was let go, the historical record does not include mention of a sexual relationship between Proctor and Abigail. Much of what is depicted in the play, however, actually happened in Salem.

The events covered in the play occurred in Salem Village between January and September, 1692. Witchcraft trials were not new to the area, however. In 1688 Goody Glover, a laundress in nearby Boston, was convicted and hanged by Reverend Cotton Mather for bewitching thirteen-year-old Martha Goodwin, her younger brother, and her two sisters. That same year, Mather, who was the model for Miller's character Reverend Hale, wrote a book about the incident, entitled *Memorable Providences, Relating to Witchcraft.*

In 1692 the real Abigail Williams was only eleven years old, and Betty Parris was only nine. A few years before, Betty's father, Samuel Parris, had been hired by influential town elder John Putnam to preach in the local church. Parris, who had previously worked as a merchant in Barbados, lived in the village with his wife; daughter; servant, Tituba; and orphan niece, Abigail.

Historians point out that at the time of the witch trials, Massachusetts colonists were waging war against hostile Native Americans and were adjusting to a changing economic and social structure. In Salem the Putnam family was competing with the Porter clan for control of the village. The hiring of Parris as minister was as much a political move as a religious one, and at the time of the trials, Parris's position in the village was precarious.

In early 1692, during a particularly cold winter, Betty Parris began behaving strangely and complained of fever, much as Martha Goodwin had in 1688. Soon after, Abigail also became afflicted with a mysterious ailment. When the children failed to respond to his treatments, the village doctor suggested that witchcraft might be involved. At the request of neighbor Mary Sibley, Tituba made a "witch cake" from dog urine, following an old English folk remedy. She then fed the cake to the dog, hoping to reverse whatever spell had been placed on the girls.

The remedy did not help, and Betty finally identified Tituba as the cause of her odd behavior. As a black woman known for her West Indian superstitions and voodoo practices, Tituba was an obvious target for the girls. Betty and Abigail also accused Sarah Good and Sarah Osburn of witchcraft, and arrest warrants were issued for the three women. As depicted in the play, Tituba confessed to practicing witchcraft and claimed Good and Osburn as her accomplices. Good was a known beggar, and Osburn was bad-tempered and did not attend church.

Soon after, John Putnam's daughter, Ann, began acting strangely and accused elderly Martha Corey of witchcraft. Ann and her friend Mercy Lewis presented the first "spectral" evidence of witchcraft, claiming to have seen witches flying through the mist. More girls became "afflicted," and a wave of accusations and arrests followed. Abigail identified Rebecca Nurse as a witch, and in late March, Elizabeth Proctor, John's wife, was accused of witchcraft by their servant, Mary Warren. In April, Mary retracted her statement and accused the other girls of lying.

Despite Mary's admission, more villagers were implicated as witches, including a former Salem minister. Sarah Osburn died in prison in May. In June,

Bridget Bishop became the first woman to be hanged for practicing witchcraft. Cotton Mather then wrote a cautionary letter to the Salem court, requesting that spectral evidence not be used and the accused be given speedy trials.

Mather's request was generally ignored. In July, Rebecca Nurse and several other women were hanged at Gallows Hill. Soon after, Elizabeth Proctor was found guilty but was spared hanging because she was pregnant.

The trials and hangings continued for another two months. Giles Corey died as depicted in the play—crushed by the weight of rocks after refusing to confess. In late October the governor of Massachusetts, having declared spectral evidence inadmissible, ordered an end to the arrests and released many of the accused.

In the end, nineteen men and women, including John Proctor, were hanged for witchcraft, and one hundred to two hundred more were arrested and jailed. Four of the accused died in prison while await-ing judgment. In 1697 Parris was voted out of office and left Salem for good. After Abigail took off, rumors began circulating that she had become a prostitute in Boston. Tituba was sold to a new master, and Elizabeth remarried four years after Proctor's death.

Although Ann Putnam publicly apologized in 1706,

most of the judges refused to admit any wrongdoing. In 1711 the colony passed a bill restoring the rights of the accused and awarded their heirs a significant sum of money. The farms of some of the accused, however, were abandoned and left in ruins for over one hundred years. In 1992, three hundred years after the trials, the state of Massachusetts formally apologized for the witch hunt.

THEMES

Although stylistically *The Crucible* bears little resemblance to Miller's earlier plays, especially *Death of a Salesmen*, thematically it is similar. Like the earlier plays, *The Crucible* examines how man's responsibility to himself and his family sometimes conflicts with his responsibility to society. The Proctors' problem, namely Proctor's adultery, conflicts with the family's duties as citizens of Salem. To protect his community from hysterical injustice, Proctor needs to expose the reason behind Abigail's lies, but to do that, he must implicate himself as a sinner.

During the first two acts Proctor struggles with that decision, admitting the truth only after Elizabeth is arrested. When he finally confesses his sin in public, he does so primarily to protect his wife, not others who have been arrested. He disapproves of the witch hunt, but does not feel compelled to officially decry it.

Like Joe Keller in *All My Sons*, Proctor at first views his personal needs as distinct from his community's.

In the final act, however, Proctor gradually comes to understand that he cannot separate himself from the world. At first, he is willing to lie that he consorted with witches. When Danforth demands his signed confession, however, Proctor imagines the document displayed in public and says, "I have three children—how may I teach them to walk like men in the world, and I sold my friends? . . . I blacken all of them when this is nailed to the church the very day they hang for silence!"[8] No doubt Miller was thinking of Kazan when he wrote these lines, and was imagining how his own name might look "nailed" before the public's eyes.

Guilt is another familiar theme used in the play. Like Willy Loman, Proctor feels guilt for breaking his marriage vows, and like Joe Keller, he feels guilt for hiding the truth. Unlike the earlier protagonists, however, Proctor recognizes his sins as sins from the beginning, and acknowledges them, first to his wife and then to the court. And unlike Keller, Proctor goes to his death, not out of guilt and shame, but as an act of contrition.

Guilt is also the motivating force in the development of Mary, Hale, and Parris. While Hale seems genuinely remorseful, Parris's and Mary's change of heart occur only after their position and safety are threatened. Mary finally gives in to Abigail, while Parris ends a broken man.

Related to the theme of guilt is the theme of public ritual. In *Timebends*, Miller wrote about the HUAC-Salem connection:

> Whatever else they might be, I saw that the hearings in Washington were profoundly and even avowedly ritualistic. . . . The main point of the hearings, precisely as in seventeenth-century Salem, was that the accused make public confession, damn his confederates as well as his Devil master, and guarantee his sterling new allegiance by breaking disgusting old vows.[9]

Miller points out that like McCarthy and HUAC, the Salem judges had already convicted the people that they wanted others, like Proctor, to accuse in writing. The purpose of Proctor's confession is not to reveal a new truth but to "purge" his soul and prove its pureness to the community. In this way, Miller argues, the witch trials were more about superstition than justice.

Similarly, the trials revealed Salem's corruption of power, another theme explored in *The Crucible*. In seventeenth-century Massachusetts, the Christian church played a key role in the governing of the colonies, and strictly religious matters, like Devil worship, were deemed crimes punishable by the courts.

There was little separation between what today would be considered personal matters—sexual and religious practices, for example—and public concern. Consequently, when Proctor questions the existence of witches, he is, in effect, challenging the power structure and is, therefore, viewed with suspicion.

Miller shows how easily power based on superstition, suspicion, and repression, as opposed to reason and fact, can be corrupted. By the end of act three, Salem's children, usually the least powerful members of society, have acquired unquestioned authority. Other citizens, like the Putnams, have been rewarded for tattling on neighbors and friends.

In their zeal to squash the Devil and exert their power, the judges and reverends of Salem create hysteria. Instead of protecting the community, they plunge it into chaos.

CHARACTERS

In his introduction to the revised 1958 version of *The Crucible*, theater scholar Richard Watts, Jr., complains that Miller's characters seem like "dramatized points of view, rather than full-length, fully rounded human beings."[10]

Certainly the characters of *The Crucible* are psychologically less complex than those in *Death of a*

Salesman. Their relative simplicity, however, fits the type of drama Miller sets out to create.

John Proctor

The word "crucible" can be defined as a severe, searching test or trial. In Miller's play the crucible belongs to John Proctor. Some critics have pointed out that with Proctor, Miller had his first real "hero" protagonist. Proctor is, in fact, more courageous than any of the Kellers or the Lomans. He is, however, a flawed hero.

In his revised stage directions Miller describes the real John Proctor as "powerful of body, even-tempered, and not easily led." He also defines Proctor as a "sinner, not only against the moral fashion of the time, but against his own vision of decent conduct."[11] Proctor not only commits adultery but also hesitates to expose Abigail until it is too late. Danforth suspects that Proctor is admitting to adultery only to save Elizabeth, which, in effect, is true.

To justify his desire to confess bewitchment, Proctor tells Elizabeth he is unworthy of dying like a "saint," as he is a fraud—a man who has not earned the respect others give him. Unlike the truly fraudu-lent Willy Loman, however, Proctor recognizes his chance to be heroic and seizes his opportunity. He dies virtuous.

101

Elizabeth Proctor

With Elizabeth, Miller creates yet another strong, self-sacrificing wife. Unlike Kate of *All My Sons* and Linda of *Death of a Salesman*, though, Elizabeth's moral vision is crystal clear. She loves Proctor and, as an expectant mother, needs him, but she accepts that he has to sacrifice himself for the greater good.

Like Proctor, Elizabeth is not without flaws and contradictory traits. She is both tender—she expresses sorrow for having killed a rabbit for dinner, for example—and harsh. She is slow to forgive Proctor for his adultery but is willing to lie for him.

At the end, she admits she may have driven Proctor into Abigail's arms because she did not express her love for him. "I counted myself so plain," she says, "so poorly made, no honest love could come to me! Suspicion kissed you when I did; I never knew how I should say my love."[12] Like Proctor's, Elizabeth's character grows, from self-pity and self-doubt to insight and courage.

Abigail, Danforth, and Hathorne

Abigail, Danforth, and Hathorne represent Miller's first truly villainous characters. Danforth and Hathorne are motivated by ambition and pride, and Abigail is driven by jealousy and lust. Miller describes Hathorne as "bitter and remorseless" and Danforth as "grave." Danforth sees the witch hunt as a way to increase his power and insists that the trials continue, even after other officials, like Hale, begin to question their legitimacy.

Abigail is a more subtle character than Danforth or Hathorne but is equally influential in the play's conflict. Miller gives Abigail physical beauty but spiritual blankness. Although Danforth and the other judges are the only ones who can actually condemn and punish, it is Abigail, as the leader of the girls, who pushes the story with her unrelenting desire.

In the earliest version of the play, Miller included a brief night scene between Proctor and Abigail at the end of act two. In the scene Proctor has secretly summoned Abigail to meet him in the forest and threatens to ruin her unless she confesses her deception. Undeterred, Abigail demands that Proctor resist the hypocrisy of their society and admit that he loves her.

Describing her as a frustrated, lost child, Miller creates some sympathy for Abigail in this scene and allows her to speak hard truths about Proctor and the village. After going back and forth about whether to keep the scene in the play, Miller finally chose to delete it, and it is rarely seen in American productions (although it was included in some published editions and in the filmed version). Without it Abigail is a fiercer antagonist—less subtle but dramatically more powerful.

The single-mindedness of all these antagonists provides the play with its force. Their corruption provides the necessary foil to the decency of the victims. In real life, Danforth and Hathorne were as vicious and determined as Miller portrays them. In his notes Miller informs the reader that some of the judges and accusers never accepted responsibility or expressed remorse for their actions.

Hale and Parris

In many aspects Reverends Hale and Parris are typical Miller characters, confused and conflicted. When we first see Parris in the play's opening, he is genuinely distraught at his daughter's illness, praying and weeping over her. In the end, he feels no remorse but, like Willy Loman, is bewildered and terrified by the results of his actions. The scholarly Hale begins confident but eventually is filled with doubt. He is a man betrayed by his learning, who, while sympathetic, fails to see the light.

LANGUAGE

According to Miller biographer Gottfried, Miller first wrote *The Crucible* in verse. Writing in verse helped

Miller create seventeenth-century speech that was believable, but not stilted. Although the vocabulary and syntax of *The Crucible* are historically accurate, the dialogue is still stylized.

Characters in *The Crucible* do not have catch-phrases, but certain words are used often and take on symbolic meaning in the text. Many of them relate to the physical senses, especially the sense of touch, but also sight and sound. Miller uses these words to suggest hidden and suppressed impulses, impulses that bewitchment and Devil worship were believed to unleash.

A scene from the 1953 stage production of *The Crucible*, as staged by Jed Harris.

The words "soft" and "soften," for example, are used repeatedly in different ways in the play. Early on, Abigail asks Proctor to give her a "soft" word, that is, be romantic with her. In act two Hale accuses Proctor of "softness" in regards to his church attendance. Here, the word "softness" suggests a lack of discipline and resolve. Hale questions whether Proctor is truly committed to fighting the Devil or has become "soft" in his defense. In the last act Danforth asks whether Rebecca and Martha have "softened," or weakened, in their resolve not to confess.

The word "cold" also appears many times throughout the text. According to Hale, cold skin and feeling a cold wind are signs of demonic possession. "Icy," "cool" and "coolness" are used to describe the various effects of the girls' bewitchment. In other places in the text, however, "cold" means unloving. Abigail describes Elizabeth as a "cold" wife, and at the end of the play, Elizabeth blames herself for keeping a "cold" home.

In contrast to the "cold" references, Miller's text also boasts many images of fire and burning. These images suggest biblical damnation on both social and personal levels. According to Puritan church doctrine, unrepentant sinners—like the villagers found guilty of witchcraft or the adulterous Proctor—are doomed to burn in hell. And while the Salem condemned were hanged in public, unconfessed witches in Europe were often burned at the stake.

The first and perhaps most powerful reference to fire in the play can be found in the title. In addition to its meaning as a severe test or trial, a crucible can also be defined as a container for heating substances to high temperatures. The village, the Proctor household, and the Salem courthouse all function as containers holding highly combustible, emotional material.

Other fire images are sprinkled throughout the play. In act one Ann Putnam, in justifying her claims of witchcraft, comments: "There are wheels within wheels in this village, and fires within fires!"[13] Danforth says of the official investigation: "We burn a hot fire here; it melts down all concealment."[14] The most dramatic fire image in the play, however, is uttered by a frenzied Proctor at the end of act three: "A fire, a fire is burning! I hear the boot of Lucifer! I see his filthy face! . . . God damns our kind especially, and we will burn, we will burn together."[15]

THEATRICAL STYLE

Interestingly, although *The Crucible* is based on real legal proceedings, none of the action is set in the courtroom proper. Instead, the drama unfolds in smaller, more intimate settings. Many of the production details echo the symbolism of the dialogue. Miller describes the seventeenth-century rooms and furniture as "low," "raw," "narrow," "heavy," "forbidding," and "unmellowed," terms that hint at the play's themes of oppression. Not surprisingly, the jail set is dominated by bars and darkness.

Miller often uses light and darkness metaphorically, or symbolically, in his plays, and windows are an important feature in the sets of *The Crucible*. Light suggests purity, strength, truth, and knowledge; darkness suggests ignorance and impurity. In his stage directions Miller indicates that either sunlight or moonlight is to stream through the various windows.

METAPHOR—*A figure of speech in which a comparison is made between two words or phrases that have no literal relationship.*

At times, the light is obstructed by bars or is forced through high, narrow openings. Like truth, light in *The Crucible* struggles to be seen. The last image of the play is of Elizabeth, gripping the bars of the jail's window as a "new sun is pouring in upon her face."[16] This fresh light signals not only Proctor's soul cleansing before death but also the triumph of courage over cowardice, knowledge over ignorance.

THE PRICE OF FAME

CHAPTER 6

A View from the Bridge, After the Fall, Incident at Vichy, and The Price

After *The Crucible*, Miller's life became dominated by personal and political travails. In 1956 he divorced Mary and married Marilyn Monroe, the most famous movie actress of the day. Although *Death of a Salesman* had brought Miller a certain amount of public recognition, it paled in comparison to Monroe's fame. Miller, a private, almost reclusive man, had to adjust to living in a "fishbowl" with a film icon. Despite her fun-loving, on-screen persona, Monroe suffered from mental illness and addiction, and the two struggled to make the marriage work.

At the same time, Miller was ordered to appear before HUAC. When he wrote *The Crucible* in the early 1950s, Miller had been only indirectly affected by

America's communist witch hunt. Believing their impact on the public was nominal, HUAC had expressed little interest in pursuing theater professionals, concentrating instead on moviemakers.

By the mid-1950s, however, the committee had branched out. When he was finally called to testify before HUAC, Miller refused to identify his friends and fellow writers, and in 1957 he was convicted of contempt of Congress. The conviction was overturned in 1958, and Miller never served any jail time.

Distracted by his marital problems and HUAC, Miller's literary output declined during the late 1950s and early 1960s. In 1956 *A View from the Bridge*, which Miller first wrote as a one-act play, opened in London. The story, set on the New York waterfront, had been brewing in Miller's mind for a long time. Although not as autobiographical as some of his other plays, it still contains themes and situations dear to Miller's heart.

The play's main character, dockworker Eddie Carbone, is living with his wife, Beatrice, and orphaned niece, Catherine, in postwar Brooklyn when two of his wife's cousins, Rodolpho and Marco, emigrate illegally from Italy. Eddie agrees to house his in-laws, but after the younger, handsome Rodolpho begins a romance with Catherine, Eddie fills with jealousy. Although Eddie knows his attraction for

Catherine is taboo, he cannot control his emotions and ends up betraying Rodolpho and Marco to the authorities. Eddie's neighbors and coworkers condemn him as a traitor, and Marco kills him in a fight.

A View from the Bridge expresses both Miller's thoughts about poor immigrant communities and his feelings about destructive lust and betrayal, the kind of betrayal Miller encountered with HUAC and Elia Kazan. The play's themes are connected by a narrator character, a lawyer who comments on the action and acts as a sounding board for Eddie's conscience. As is typical in Miller's work, Eddie's community has a key role in the conflict. Miller noted in his introduction to the play: "The mind of Eddie Carbone is not comprehensible apart from its relation to his neighborhood, his fellow workers, his social situation."[1]

The successful London production of *A View from the Bridge* was significant in that it marked the beginning of Miller's popularity in Great Britain, an appreciation that continues to this day. In America, however, Miller's star was falling. The one-act version of *A View from the Bridge*, presented in 1955 with *A Memory of Two Mondays*, had flopped, and *The Misfits*, the 1961 movie he wrote for Monroe, first published as a short story in 1957, died at the box office. By then, his marriage had fallen apart, and he and Monroe divorced before the movie's premiere.

111

Arthur Miller escorts his then-wife Marilyn Monroe down the red carpet at the movie premiere of *The Prince and the Showgirl* that took place at New York's Radio City Music Hall on June 13, 1957.

Miller quickly remarried. His third wife, Inge Morath, was an Austrian-born photographer who had worked while a political prisoner in a dangerous German airplane factory during World War II. Morath, with whom Miller had two children, provided the playwright with a stable home life, and Miller returned to writing in earnest. In 1963 his children's book, *Jane's Blanket*, was published, and in 1964 two plays, *After the Fall* and *Incident at Vichy*, opened in New York.

With its thinly veiled portrayal of Monroe, who had just died from a drug overdose, *After the Fall* caused an uproar in America. Quentin, the play's unhappy protagonist, seemed obviously based on Miller, and the supporting characters, including Maggie, the Monroe stand-in, came straight out of his past. Stylistically, the drama resembles *Death of a Salesman*, going back and forth in time from inside Quentin's memory and imagination. Although Miller reunited with Kazan for the project, the director chose to emphasize the Monroe angle, and the play was severely criticized in the press.

Incident at Vichy was Miller's first play about Nazi Germany and marked his return to the theme of anti-Semitism. Like *All My Sons*, the play was inspired by a tale told to Miller by an acquaintance. In 1942 a friend of this friend, a Jew who was living in Vichy,

France, was rounded up by Nazis and taken to a police station. There, he joined a group of other men waiting in line to be questioned by Vichy police. After being called in to the office, some of the men left the station, but most never reemerged.

In an essay about the play, Miller described the fate of his friend's friend:

> As he got closer and closer to the fatal door he became more and more certain that his death was near. Finally, there was only one man between him and that door. Presently, this last man was ordered into the office. . . . The door opened. The man who had been the last to go in came out. . . . But instead of walking past him with his pass to freedom, the Gentile who had just come out stopped in front of my friend's friend, thrust his pass into his hand, and whispered for him to go. He went.[2]

The play *Incident at Vichy* follows the friend's story closely, focusing on a diverse group of men awaiting interrogation at a Nazi-run police station. The men suspect that the Nazis have brought them in to determine their ethnicity, and they know that if they are identified as Jewish, they will be shipped to a death camp. One by one, as the strangers await their interrogation, their hatreds and fears are revealed. In the end, however, a Gentile nobleman puts aside his prejudices and sacrifices his future for a Jew.

Rich with Miller's favorite themes, *Incident at*

Vichy was more traditional and accessible than *After the Fall*, but it, too, failed at the box office. Critics blasted the play for being too contrived and outdated in its theatrical style. In early 1967 Miller published a collection of short stories called *I Don't Need You Anymore*, and *The Price*, his next play, opened in 1968.

Like *Incident at Vichy*, *The Price* is a compact, straightforward drama that unfolds in real time. In other words, the action of the story and the time it takes to present the action are more or less equal.

The Price, which had begun life as Miller's "third play," is set in contemporary Brooklyn. Two grown brothers, Walter and Victor, reunite after years of silence to sell their dead father's furniture. Policeman Victor resents his older brother for going off to medical school, leaving Victor to work and take care of his father, a businessman devastated by the Depression. As Gregory Solomon, an ancient furniture dealer, watches with amusement, Victor and Walter argue about their father and the family secrets that have driven them apart.

The Price explores many of Miller's favorite themes—guilt, family, social responsibility—and contains many autobiographical elements. Victor and Walter are somewhat similar to Miller and his brother, Kermit, with whom Miller had a loving but competitive relationship. The characters also echo Miller and his close childhood friend, Sid Franks, who like Victor became a policeman because of family financial problems and never fulfilled his intellectual promise.

Although not as successful as *Death of a Salesmen*, *The Price*, which opened in New York on February 7, 1968, enjoyed good reviews and a healthy run. It would be a long time before Miller would again be so appreciated in his own country.

FROM THE PAGE TO THE STAGE

Theatrical presentation of Miller's texts

In the introduction to his collected plays, Arthur Miller observed about his dramas:

> These plays were written on the assumption that they would be acted before audiences. The "actor" is a person, and he no sooner appears than certain elementary questions are broached. Who is he? What is he doing here? How does he live or make his living? Who is he related to? Is he rich or poor? What does he think of himself? What do other people think of him, and why?. . . The actor brings questions onto the stage just as any person does when we first meet him in our ordinary lives.[1]

As any playwright knows, how well a play is produced is just as important to its success as how well it is written. During rehearsals the text of a play can go through many changes. With each new production the writer is directly involved in, the play will likely be rewritten, at least a little. In many cases, the first production of a play can determine its commercial fate, for better or worse. Over the decades Miller has experienced both the joy of a great production and the disappointment of an inferior one.

In addition to actors, many artists—set designers, directors, costumers, and others—contribute to a play's production. Before and during rehearsals playwrights, particularly on first productions, work closely with these collaborators. Often, in response to questions raised by the director or the actors, playwrights will rework parts of the text or cut or expand certain scenes.

CASTING

Casting is perhaps the single most important element of a theatrical production. Actors are an extension of the playwright, adding, in effect, the final touch to the writer's voice. Even the smallest movements, vocal quirks, and expressions of actors can affect how their characters are perceived. Miller sometimes anticipated differences in actors and their performances. In his opening directions to *The Price*, for example, Miller noted that how the part of older brother Walter was interpreted would determine how sympathetic the audience would be to his development.

Good casting was a crucial element in the initial

success of *Death of a Salesman* and actually led to changes in Miller's text. Originally Miller conceived of Willy as a small man, like his uncle Manny. Lee J. Cobb, who played Willy in the Broadway premiere, was tall and bulky. After he was cast, Miller changed a line in the play to accommodate Cobb's size. Instead of describing himself as "shrimp," Willy complains about being "fat" and "foolish to look at."

Critics agree that casting a large actor in the role of Willy enhanced the drama. Although smaller men, such as Dustin Hoffman, have successfully played the role, it is generally regarded as a large man's part. As Miller biographer Gottfried observed: "To watch a grown man fall apart is painful enough, but when he is physically imposing, it becomes pitiful."[2]

Who picks a play's cast? Generally a play's director and sometimes its producer will confer with the playwright about casting. Playwrights will sometimes write a role with a particular actor in mind or cast the same actor in similar roles in different plays. For example, stage and screen actor Arthur Kennedy played Chris in *All My Sons*, Biff in *Death of a Salesman*, John Proctor in *The Crucible*, and Walter in *The Price*.

STAGING

Once a play has been cast and rehearsals begin, the director takes over. In deciding how actors are to be blocked—how, when, and where they are to move on the stage—directors can draw the audience's attention toward or away from a given character or moment. That drawing, in turn, can affect how the audience reacts to a character, and ultimately how the audience reacts to the drama as a whole.

Directors also guide the lighting, set, sound, and costume designers, helping them find the right complement to the story's themes and action. As previously noted, directors can sometimes drastically alter the playwright's stage directions or interpret them in fanciful ways. When *The Crucible* was first produced in the Soviet Union, for instance, the director had the actor playing John Proctor chased by a mob wearing balloon pants and carrying scimitars.

THE KAZAN FACTOR

Besides the play itself, teaming with director Elia Kazan on *All My Sons* may have been the single most important event in Miller's career. Along with his theatrical partner, producer-director Harold Clurman, Kazan was a graduate of New York's pioneering Group Theatre and brought with him years of directing experience. At the time of *All My Sons*, Kazan had already begun directing movies, including the hugely successful *A Tree Grows in Brooklyn* (1945). His personal and artistic sensibilities were very different from Miller's, but this opposition brought out qualities in Miller's texts that might otherwise have gone unnoticed. Kazan's overall impact on Miller and his work was significant.

Before starting to rehearse one of Miller's plays, Kazan would go over every detail of the script, taking notes about the characters' psychology and background—their likes, dislikes, fears, needs, and so on. On *All My Sons*, for example, Kazan noted about mother Kate: "She would not only lie to keep Larry and Chris safe. She would kill. Don't underestimate either her cunning, her strength or her ferocity. Kate and Keller are two tough hombres, no joke."[3]

Based on his character observations, Kazan would sometimes make suggestions for line changes or additions. For instance, to sharpen Happy's character in *Death of a Salesman*, Kazan suggested Miller make him vain, and Miller responded by adding Happy's catchphrase, "I lost weight, Pop."

Kazan then would devise an attack for directing each scene and a structure for the play as a whole. For *All My Sons*, Kazan concluded that the story's center lay in the relationship between Chris and his father, Keller. Kazan directed each scene to highlight the father-son conflict. According to Gottfried, it was at "Kazan's urging that Miller toned down the

Playwright Tennessee Williams, director Elia Kazan, and Arthur Miller (left to right) at an event held at Brentano's bookstore in New York in February 1967.

mother's powerful effect to allow for the conflict between Chris and Keller."[4]

Kazan increased the play's tension through his aggressive blocking, which had the actors in one another's faces from the outset. Gottfried noted that Kazan's staging of *All My Sons* "was so intense that audiences seemed to fear for a son striking his father even before it happened."[5] Kazan's dynamic movements brought out the subtext of Miller's speech, that is, the emotions hidden under the dialogue.

Like most theater directors, Kazan would give actors bits of stage business—small actions, such as wiping down a table or carrying a newspaper—he believed added to a character's portrayal. Based on his reading of *All My Sons*, for example, Kazan concluded that Joe Keller was very frugal and would bring home scraps of material he found on the street. For *Death of a Salesman*, Kazan insisted that Willy be first seen carrying two heavy suitcases to suggest the weight of his troubles. The image of a man bent over and lugging suitcases became synonymous with Willy's character.

The memory scenes in *Death of a Salesman* presented Kazan with a special directing challenge. In particular, Kazan had to help the actors negotiate the time shifts, while respecting the fluidity of the text. Kazan instructed the actors to play their past selves as Willy imagines them to be, idealized in his mind, in contrast to their present-day real selves. For Willy's brother Ben, who has no present-day scenes, Kazan suggested the actor wear exaggerated "adventurer" clothes—whips, spurs, flashy jewelry, hats, and boots. Ben's costume helped both the actor and the audience to understand the mysterious character.

Because of scheduling conflicts, Kazan could not direct *The Crucible*, and Broadway veteran Jed Harris was hired. In many ways, Harris was the opposite of Kazan. Instead of dynamic staging, he stuck the actors in one spot, posing them like subjects in a painting. He encouraged them to make speeches to the audience instead of talking to one another. The end result was a slow, stiff play, "cold," as the critics—and Miller himself—described it.

MILLER AND HIS CONTEMPORARIES

Eugene O'Neill, Clifford Odets, Tennessee Williams, and Samuel Beckett

In his introduction to the book *The Theater Essays of Arthur Miller*, Miller scholar Robert A. Martin described the playwright's contributions this way: "Along with the plays of Eugene O'Neill and Tennessee Williams, Arthur Miller's plays have been responsible in large part for extending the significance of the American theater beyond the horizons of its national origins, and for providing a standard of dramatic achievement."[1] With plays like *Death of a Salesman*, the theatrical landscape that had been defined by early-twentieth-century writers such as O'Neill and Clifford Odets began to change. Miller was both positively influenced by his immediate predecessors and repulsed by them. He both emulated them and rejected them.

Likewise, Miller's contemporaries (dramatists producing work during the same period as Miller) echoed his efforts and at the same time departed

125

from them. In addition to Miller's work, drama of the late twentieth century was dominated by the very different talents of Tennessee Williams, Samuel Beckett, and Edward Albee.

EUGENE O'NEILL

Eugene O'Neill (1888–1953), who like Miller was born in New York City and lived in Connecticut, is best known for his lyrical, autobiographical dramas. When Miller first read O'Neill as a college student during the mid-1930s, he viewed him as old-fashioned and stuffy. At that time O'Neill's work, including a series of nine plays about a New England family, was highly impressionistic and often featured well-to-do characters.

Years later Miller came to appreciate O'Neill's "radical hostility to bourgeois civilization."[2] In 1946 Miller saw a production of O'Neill's drama *The Iceman Cometh* (completed in 1940 but not produced until 1946) and was struck by the seamless way O'Neill had presented ordinary people in a larger social context. Set in a bar, *The Iceman Cometh* features a down-and-out salesman character, not unlike Willy Loman. O'Neill's salesman, however, is a less realized character than Willy, functioning more as a symbol than a three-dimensional protagonist.

As Miller's theatrical career was taking off,

O'Neill's was ending. Because of illness, O'Neill failed to produce a completed work after 1944, although his reputation was already in decline by that time. In all, O'Neill received four Pulitzer Prizes and was the first American to win the Nobel Prize for Literature. His most famous play, *Long Day's Journey into Night*, completed in 1940, was not produced until 1956, three years after his death.

CLIFFORD ODETS

Miller first met Clifford Odets (1906–1963) in a New York bookstore in 1940. Odets's literary career, as well as his public life, overlapped Miller's for over a decade, although like O'Neill, Odets's star was falling while Miller's was rising. Like Miller, Odets, who was a founding member of the Group Theatre, made his name writing about the underprivileged. His first plays, *Waiting for Lefty* and *Awake and Sing!*, both produced in 1935, reflected his communist leanings and won him much critical acclaim.

Waiting for Lefty, whose original cast included Elia Kazan, dramatized trade union corruption. *Awake and Sing!*, about an extended Jewish family in the Bronx battling poverty and repression, reflected both Odets's upbringing and his politics. According to Miller, Odets's plays represented "a new phenomenon, a leftish challenge to the system, but even more, the poet suddenly leaping onto the stage and disposing of middle-class gentility, screaming and yelling and cursing like somebody off the Manhattan streets. For the very first time in America, language itself had marked a playwright as unique."[3]

Miller was inspired by the young Odets, who was also a friend of Kazan. With his overtly political plays and challenging use of language, Odets forged the way for Miller. In the early 1940s, however, Odets went to Los Angeles and began writing screenplays, and Miller, who had resisted the pull of Hollywood, sensed a decline in the quality of his work and a hypocrisy behind his politics.

In 1953 Odets, who had joined the Communist Party in 1934, was called to testify before HUAC. According to Miller's autobiography, Odets and Kazan had made an agreement to name each other to the committee, and Odets became a "friendly" witness. Although not blacklisted, Odets was traumatized by his HUAC experience and stopped writing drama after 1954.

TENNESSEE WILLIAMS

Besides Miller, no other playwright defined American theater in the mid- to late-twentieth century more than Tennessee Williams (1911–1983). Like many of Miller's dramas, Williams's plays focused on the family and were intensely autobiographical, mining the more intimate details of his Southern upbringing. His first major work, *A Glass Menagerie*, was produced in 1944 and won a New York Drama Critics' Circle Award for best play.

His most famous play, *A Streetcar Named Desire*, opened in late 1947, almost a year after Miller's *All My Sons*. *Streetcar* stunned audiences with its daring examination of such taboo sexual issues as homosexuality and nymphomania. The homosexual Williams dared audiences to emphasize with his broken, misfit characters. Like Willy Loman, the protagonists of *Streetcar*, Blanche DuBois and Stanley Kowalski, would become icons of American theater.

Kazan directed the Pulitzer Prize–winning *Streetcar*, as well as the movie adaptation, which was released in 1951. Williams's professional relationship with Kazan was in many ways similar to Miller's. After seeing the show in its pre-Broadway run, Miller declared that Williams had "opened one specific door for me. Not the story or characters or direction, but the words and their liberation, the joy of the writer in writing them, the radiant eloquence of its composition, moved me more than all its pathos."[4]

Williams and Miller were both midcentury drama pioneers, but their work reflects fundamental artistic differences. Although Williams's plays had a social

Arthur Miller stands at the intersection of New York's West 49th Street and Broadway on February 3, 1999. The street was temporarily renamed "Arthur Miller Way" in celebration of the fiftieth anniversary of *Death of a Salesman*.

component, they were less political than Miller's. Miller's dramas were less lyrical and stylized than Williams's, but structurally they were more complex and daring. Both writers, however, probed deep into the human psyche.

Marked by such plays as *Cat on a Hot Tin Roof* (1955) and *Night of the Iguana* (1961), Williams's career soared all through the 1950s and early 1960s. By the late 1960s, however, Williams slowed down, the victim of depression and addiction. He continued to write until his death in 1983, but his output and popularity waned. As he did with Odets and so many other playwrights, Miller outlasted his favorite theatrical rival.

SAMUEL BECKETT

In a 1999 survey of theater professionals conducted by the Royal National Theatre of Great Britain, *Death of a Salesman* was named the second most significant English-language play of the twentieth century, and *The Crucible* the sixth. Number one was *Waiting for Godot* by Samuel Beckett (1906–1989). Although *Waiting for Godot* opened in France in 1953, the same year as *The Crucible*, the two plays could not have been more different, and Miller and the Irish-born Beckett could not have been more different in their writing style and philosophy. Both playwrights, however, have an equally important place in the history of twentieth-century dramatic literature.

When *Waiting for Godot* first opened in New York in 1956, Miller criticized the play for abandoning the fundamentals of dramatic writing. Despite initial rejection by Miller and American critics, the drama not only endured but ushered in a new type of dramatic art called theater of the absurd. Absurdist plays are characterized by nonrepresentational, or symbolic, settings and odd, illogical plot action. While more traditional dramas focus on characters with specific histories and problems, absurdist plays explore the problem of being human in the most general sense.

ABSURDISM—*The philosophical and literary doctrine that people live in isolation in a meaningless and nonsensical world.*

NONREPRESENTATIONAL—*Not depicting an object in a recognizable manner.*

Beckett is known for his stark portrayals of lonely people trying to make sense out of a senseless world. Society and family do not exist in Beckett's world, only individuals thrown together in strange landscapes. Beckett's plays have no real character or plot development. Instead, they unfurl like a series of dramatic snapshots.

Just as *Death of a Salesman* had blown apart some of the conventions of Broadway theater when it first opened, *Waiting for Godot* challenged standards set by such dramatists as Miller and Tennessee Williams. With *Endgame* (1957), *Krapp's Last Tape* (1958), and *Happy Days* (1961), Beckett questioned not only what it means to be human but also what it means to be an artist.

Over time, Beckett's plays became more and more spare and brief. Late in his career, Beckett invented his own theatrical format called dramaticules. One of these extremely short pieces, *Come and Go*, was only forty-five seconds long. Beckett, who received the Nobel Prize for Literature in 1969, also wrote fiction, poems, and teleplays.

EDWARD ALBEE

Like Miller, Edward Albee (1928–) was a product of the New York theater scene. At twenty Albee, who had been adopted as an infant by a well-to-do couple, rejected his family's status and wealth and struck out on his own. Just as Miller had, Albee worked at a number of odd jobs, including office boy and record salesman. He also wrote music programming for a New York radio station before his interest turned to playwriting.

In 1958 Albee's one-act play *The Zoo Story* opened in Berlin, Germany. On the same bill as Samuel Beckett's *Krapp's Last Tape*, *The Zoo Story* told the tale of a drifter who enacts his own murder. A year later the same double bill was produced off-Broadway in New York. This early association with Beckett fortified Albee's reputation as the first American member of the theater of the absurd.

Albee followed *The Zoo Story* with other original one-acts, including *The Death of Bessie Smith* and *The Sandbox*, as well as theatrical adaptations of fiction. In these plays Albee combined aspects of traditional American theater, exemplified by artists such as Miller and Williams, with the less realistic work of writers like Beckett.

His first three-act drama, *Who's Afraid of Virginia Woolf?*, was produced in New York in 1962. The controversial play about a combative married couple with an imaginary child, *Who's Afraid of Virginia Woolf?* won a Tony Award and was later made into a movie starring Elizabeth Taylor. In 1964 Albee became a founding member of an absurdist group called Theater 1964. Although the group had limited success in promoting theater of the absurd in America, Albee won a Pulitzer Prize for his own play *A Delicate Balance* in 1966. He won a second Pulitzer in 1975 for *Seascape*.

Like Miller, Albee, who once called Miller the "conscience" of theater, tackles social and political themes in his plays. *The Death of Bessie Smith*, for example, explores race relations, while *A Delicate Balance* questions the standards of middle-class

America. For the most part, however, Albee's writings are less realistic and more satirical, or humorously mocking, than Miller's.

During the late 1970s and 1980s Albee, like Miller, fell out of favor with the critics and experienced a long spell of commercial flops. In 1994, however, he scored a hit with his play *Three Tall Woman*, which also won him a third Pulitzer Prize. Like Miller's, Albee's career has been a long one. Forty years after the opening of *The Zoo Story*, Albee's reality-bending play *The Goat or Who Is Sylvia* opened on Broadway and won a 2002 Tony Award.

INTO THE TWENTY-FIRST CENTURY

Later works and legacy

s already noted, theater in the late 1950s and 1960s, along with other cultural institutions, went through a significant transformation. Out of the success of Samuel Beckett's *Waiting for Godot* and *Endgame* came the first plays of British playwright Harold Pinter (1930–). Though not as abstract as Beckett's plays, Pinter's *The Birthday Party* (1958) and *The Dumb Waiter* (1960) rejected the psychological and social realism typical of Miller's early work. In Pinter's plays, characters exist only in the present moment. The past—cultural, social, and personal—remains a mystery.

Like the Depression, World War II, and cold war

before them, the Vietnam War and civil rights movement had a profound effect on the arts in the late 1960s. As Miller observed in *Timebends*, "In the sixties everything one thought one knew was up for grabs."[1] Few plays in the late 1960s dealt with social and political issues in the same way that Miller's early plays had. Instead of writing about a specific event or problem, 1960s playwrights, including Albee and Sam Shepard (1943–), used absurdism to express a general disenchantment with the establishment.

The success of *The Price*, conventional by the standards of the day, proved to be the exception and not the rule for Miller in the late 1960s and 1970s. Still committed to political activism, Miller attended the 1968 Chicago Democratic Convention as a delegate, but was deeply disturbed when the event turned violent. He protested the war in Vietnam, and was in neighboring Cambodia when the first American bombs fell on the countryside.

The political and artistic turmoil of the time took its toll on Miller's creativity. Although he did produce some theater pieces, including *The Creation of the World and Other Business*, they proved slight in comparison to his earlier works. As Miller himself noted, "The compelling desire to address people, let alone entertain and enlighten them, was somehow no longer with me."[2]

Instead of drama, Miller concentrated on nonfiction, publishing three travel essay books between 1969 and 1979 with his wife, Inge Morath. In 1969 Miller wrote about the Soviet Union and the oppression of its artists in his nonfiction book *In Russia*. His 1977 play *The Archbishop's Ceiling* looked at the same subject but received little attention.

Miller also visited and wrote about Communist China in his 1979 book *Chinese Encounters*. Despite cultural and language barriers, the Chinese arts community had a special admiration for Miller, and in 1983 a Chinese language version of *Death of a Salesman*, directed by Miller himself, opened in Beijing. Miller chronicled his experience in China in his 1984 book *Salesman in Beijing*.

In 1980 Miller returned to the subject of anti-Semitism and World War II with *Playing for Time*, an adaptation of *The Musicians of Auschwitz*, the memoirs of concentration camp survivor Fania Fenelon. Miller's adaptation starred Vanessa Redgrave and was broadcast on CBS television on September 30, 1980. Miller biographer Martin Gottfried described the teleplay as "his most heartfelt Jewish expression and his most effective presentation of the survivor theme."[3]

Also in 1980, Miller created his most ambitious play to date, *The American Clock*. With its large cast and sprawling settings, *The American Clock* looked at life in the 1930s, from farmers to intellectuals to businessmen. Like *The Archbishop's Ceiling*, The *American Clock* was panned by American critics, but found a receptive audience in London.

Ironically, while Miller's new plays found appreciative audiences only in Great Britain, his reputation as America's greatest living playwright was being cemented in the United States. In 1984 Miller received a Kennedy Center lifetime achievement honor, and in 1985 a significant revival of *Death of a*

Arthur Miller appears before the Senate Judiciary Committee on April 28, 2004, to voice his support for playwright antitrust legislation.

Salesman, starring Dustin Hoffman, was broadcast on television. Also in 1985, Miller traveled to Turkey as a representative of PEN International, a writers association dedicated to promoting friendship and intellectual cooperation among writers worldwide.

In 1987, at the age of seventy-two, Miller published his autobiography, *Timebends*. Unlike most autobiographies and biographies, *Timebends* is not written chronologically. Instead, it echoes the fluidity of Willy Loman's memories, shifting back and forth in time. *Timebends* not only describes events from Miller's life but also places them within a historical context, giving the reader a broad picture of the author's world.

During the 1990s Miller wrote a number of plays, most notably *The Ride Down Mt. Morgan* and *Broken Glass*. A film version of *The Crucible*, starring Winona Ryder and Daniel Day-Lewis (who married Miller's youngest daughter, actress Rebecca Miller), was released in 1996 and earned Miller an Academy Award nomination for best adapted screenplay. In addition to *The Crucible*, many of his works have been adapted for film and television, including his novel *Focus* and plays *Death of a Salesman*, *All My Sons*, and *Incident at Vichy*.

In 2000 two collections of Miller's theater essays—*Echoes Down the Corridor* and *The Theater Essays of Arthur Miller*—were published. Although other playwrights have written about their work and about theater in general, none has scrutinized the art form to the extent that Miller did. Along with the plays themselves, these essays are an important contribution to theater history.

Miller downplayed his dramatic legacy, commenting once in a interview that his contribution to contemporary theater consisted solely of "some good parts for actors."[4] Despite this disclaimer, Miller influenced such disparate playwrights as South Africa's Athol Fugard, England's David Hare, and premiere African-American playwright August Wilson.

Until his death in early 2005, Miller spent most of his later life at his country home in Connecticut, complete with a tree farm and wildlife. To the end, he wrote everyday. His last play, *Finishing the Picture*, opened in Chicago just a few months before his death at age eighty-nine.

At the end of *Timebends*, hitting on the central theme of his art, Miller reflected on his life among the trees and coyotes: "I do not know whose land this is that I own, or whose bed I sleep in. In the darkness out there they [the coyotes] see my light and pause, muzzles lifted, wondering who I am and what I am doing here in this cabin under my light. I am a mystery to them until they tire of it and move on, but the truth, the first truth, probably, is that we are all connected, watching one another. Even the trees."[5]

CHRONOLOGY

1915—Arthur Asher Miller is born on October 17 in New York City.

1929—Father's dress business fails following the stock market crash. The Millers move to Brooklyn.

1932—Graduates from Abraham Lincoln High School.

1932–1934—Enters workforce, taking various jobs, including singing on a local radio station, truck driving, and clerking in an auto-parts warehouse.

1934–1938—Attends the University of Michigan. Studies journalism and works as a reporter and night editor on the student newspaper. In 1936 writes his first play, *No Villain*, and wins Hopwood Award in Drama. After studying playwrighting with Kenneth T. Rowe, receives his second Hopwood Award for *Honors at Dawn*. In 1938 wins second place in Hopwood contest for *The Great Disobedience*. Graduates with a B.A. in English, then moves back to New York.

1938—Joins the Federal Theater Project.

1938–1946—Writes radio plays, including several World War II propaganda scripts.

1940—Marries Mary Grace Slattery.

1941—Works as a ship fitter's helper at the Brooklyn Navy Yard.

1944—Daughter Jane is born. Is hired to write screenplay for *The Story of G.I. Joe* and tours army camps as research. Withdraws from film project but turns his research into a book entitled *Situation Normal*. First Broadway show, *The Man Who Had All the Luck*, opens and flops. Receives Theater Guild National Award.

1945—Publishes first novel, *Focus*.

1947—*All My Sons* opens and receives New York Drama Critics' Circle Award. Son, Robert, is born. Researches the Red Hook dock area of New York for possible play.

1949—*Death of a Salesman* opens and wins Pulitzer Prize, Tony Award, New York Drama Critics' Circle Award, among others.

1950—Premiere of adaptation of Ibsen's *An Enemy of the People*.

1951—Release of first film adaptation of *Death of a Salesman*, starring Frederic March.

1953—*The Crucible* opens and receives Tony Award.

1956—Divorces Mary Slattery, marries Marilyn Monroe. Is called to testify before HUAC. Revised, two-act version of *A View from the Bridge* opens in London.

1957—Convicted of contempt of Congress by HUAC for refusing to name names.

1958—United States Court of Appeals overturns contempt of Congress conviction.

1961—Divorces Marilyn Monroe. Movie *The Misfits*, starring Monroe, is released.

1962—Marries Inge Morath. Monroe dies.

1963—Daughter Rebecca is born.

1964—*After the Fall* and *Incident at Vichy* open.

1968—Premiere of *The Price*. Attends the Democratic National Convention in Chicago.

1972—*The Creation of the World and Other Business* opens.

1977—Book of reportage about Soviet Union, *In the Country*, written with Morath, published. *The Archbishop's Ceiling* opens.

1980—Premiere of *The American Clock*.

1984—Nonfiction book *Salesman in Beijing* is published. Receives Kennedy Center Honors for Lifetime Achievement.

1985—TV production of *Death of a Salesman*, starring Dustin Hoffman, broadcast on CBS.

1987—Publishes autobiography, *Timebends: A Life*.

1991—*The Ride Down Mt. Morgan* opens in London.

1994—*Broken Glass* premieres.

1998—*Mr. Peter's Connections* opens. Broadway revival of *A View from the Bridge* opens and wins two Tony Awards.

1999—*Death of a Salesman* revived on Broadway and wins Tony for Best Revival.

2001—Film adaptation of novel *Focus*, starring William Macy, is released.

2002—*The Crucible* and *The Man Who Had All the Luck* revived in New York. *Resurrection Blues* opens.

2004—*After the Fall* revived in New York. *Finishing the Picture* premieres in Chicago.

2005—Miller dies of congestive heart failure on February 10.

CHAPTER NOTES

CHAPTER 1. EVERY MAN'S PLAYWRIGHT

1. Arthur Miller, "The Price—The Power of the Past," *Echoes Down the Corridor: Collected Essays, 1944–2000* (New York: Viking Penguin, 2000), p. 299.

2. Martin Gottfried, *Arthur Miller: His Life and Work* (New York: Da Capo Press, 2003), p. xi.

3. Simi Horwitz, "Arthur Miller: On the Play, Actors and Producers," *Backstage*, November 26, 2003, <http://www.backstage.com/backstage/features/article_display.jsp?vnu_content_id=2041456> (August 13, 2004).

4. Robert A. Martin, "Introduction," *The Theater Essays of Arthur Miller*, eds. Martin and Steven R. Centola (New York: Da Capo Press, 1996), p. xxi.

5. Arthur Miller, "Foreword to *After the Fall*," *The Theater Essays of Arthur Miller*, p. 255.

6. Arthur Miller, "About Theatre Language," *The Last Yankee: with a New Essay about Theatre Language and Broken Glass* (Garden City, NY: The Fireside Theatre, 1994), p. 62.

7. Ibid., p. 70.

8. Horwitz, p. 3.

9. Miller, *The Last Yankee*, pp. 7–8.

10. Miller, "About Theatre Language," *The Last Yankee*, p. 62.

CHAPTER 2. BROADWAY-BOUND

1. Arthur Miller, "A Boy Grew in Brooklyn," *Echoes Down the Corridor: Collected Essays, 1944–2000* (New York: Viking Penguin, 2000), p. 1.

2. Arthur Miller, *Timebends: A Life* (New York: Grove Press, 1987), p. 4.

3. Ibid.

4. Ibid., p. 24.

5. Miller, "University of Michigan," *Echoes Down the Corridor*, p. 15.

6. Ibid., p. 16.

7. Miller, *Timebends*, p. 70.

CHAPTER 3. THEY WERE ALL MY SONS

1. Martin Gottfried, *Arthur Miller: His Life and Work* (New York: Da Capo Press, 2003), p. 99.

2. Arthur Miller, *Timebends: A Life* (New York: Grove Press, 1987), p. 185.

3. Arthur Miller, *All My Sons* (New York: Penguin Books, 2000), p. 89.

4. Ibid.

5. Ibid.

6. Ibid., p. 99.

7. Ibid.

8. Ibid., p. 101.

9. Ibid., p. 116.

10. Ibid., p. 117.

11. Ibid., p. 121.

12. Ibid., p. 126.

13. Ibid., p. 127.

14. Ibid., p. 135.

15. Ibid., p. 142.

16. Ibid., p. 158.

17. Ibid., p. 163.

18. Ibid., p. 169.

19. Ibid., p. 170.

20. Arthur Miller, "Introduction," *Collected Plays: One* (London: Methuen Drama, 1988), p. 19.

21. Miller, *All My Sons*, p. 118.

22. Arthur Miller, "Belief in America," *Echoes Down the Corridor: Collected Essays, 1944–2000* (New York: Viking Penguin, 2000), p. 33.

23. Miller, *All My Sons*, p. 170.

24. Ibid., p. 64.

25. Sheila Huftel, "Arthur Miller: The Burning Glass," *Readings on* All My Sons (San Diego, CA: Greenhaven Press, 2001), p. 60.

26. Miller, *Readings on* All My Sons, p. 136.

27. Ibid., p. 68.

28. Tom Scanlon, "Family, Drama and American Dreams," *Readings on* All My Sons, p. 67.

29. Miller, "Introduction," *Collected Plays: One*, p. 20.

CHAPTER 4. LIFE AND DEATH OF THE SALESMAN

1. Martin Gottfried, *Arthur Miller: His Life and Work* (New York: Da Capo Press, 2003), p. 128.

2. Arthur Miller, *Timebends: A Life* (New York: Grove Press, 1987), p. 131.

3. Ibid.

4. Ibid., p. 122.

5. Ibid., p. 129.

6. Miller, "Introduction," *Collected Plays: One* (London: Methuen Drama, 1988), p. 23.

7. Ibid., p. 23.

8. Arthur Miller, *Death of a Salesman* (New York: Penguin Books, 1998), p. 33.

9. Ibid., p. 39.

10. Ibid., p. 56.

11. Ibid., p. 81.

12. Ibid., p. 82.

13. Ibid., p. 93.

14. Ibid., p. 104.

15. Ibid., p. 126.

16. Ibid., p. 131.

17. Ibid., p. 139.

18. Arthur Miller, "The Family in Modern Drama," *The Theater Essays of Arthur Miller* (New York: Da Capo Press, 1996), p. 73.

19. Miller, *Death of a Salesman*, pp. 29–30.

20. Brian Parker, "Expressionism in *Death of a Salesman*," *Readings on* Death of a Salesman (San Diego, CA: Greenhaven Press, 1999), p. 67.

21. William Hawkins, review, *The New York*

World-Telegram, reprinted in *Death of a Salesman: Text and Criticism*, p. 202.

22. Ibid., p. 207.

23. Miller, "Tragedy and the Common Man," reprinted in *Death of a Salesman: Text and Criticism*, p. 143.

24. Miller, "Introduction," *Collected Plays: One*, p. 34.

25. Miller, "Morality and Modern Drama," *The Theater Essays of Arthur Miller*, p. 198.

26. Miller, *Death of a Salesman*, p. 81.

27. Ibid., p. 27.

28. Ibid., p. 12.

29. Ibid., p. 17.

30. Ibid., p. 36.

CHAPTER 5. CRUCIBLES

1. Arthur Miller, *The Crucible* (New York: Bantam Books, 1959), p. 60.

2. Ibid., p. 72.

3. Ibid., p. 77.

4. Ibid., p. 78.

5. Ibid., p. 106.

6. Ibid., p. 139.

7. Ibid., p. ix.

8. Ibid., p. 137.

9. Miller, *Timebends: A Life* (New York: Grove Press, 1987), p. 331.

10. Miller, *The Crucible*, p. xii.

11. Ibid., p. 18.

12. Ibid., p. 131.

13. Ibid., p. 25.

14. Ibid., p. 85.

15. Ibid., p. 115.

16. Ibid., p. 139.

CHAPTER 6. THE PRICE OF FAME

1. Arthur Miller, "Introduction to A View from the Bridge," *The Theater Essays of Arthur Miller* (New York: Da Capo Press, 1996), p. 221.

2. Arthur Miller, "Guilt and Incident at Vichy," *Echoes Down the Corridor: Collected Essays, 1944–2000* (New York: Viking Penguin, 2000), pp. 69–70.

CHAPTER 7. FROM THE PAGE TO THE STAGE

1. Arthur Miller, "Introduction," *Collected Plays: One* (London: Metheun Drama, 1988), p. 4.

2. Martin Gottfried, *Arthur Miller: His Life and Work* (New York: Da Capo Press, 2003), p. 134.

3. Ibid., p. 105.

4. Ibid., p. 106.

5. Ibid., p. 107.

CHAPTER 8. MILLER AND HIS CONTEMPORARIES

1. Robert A. Martin, "Introduction," *The Theater Essays of Arthur Miller: Collected Essays, 1944–2000* (New York: Viking Penguin, 2000), p. ix.

2. Arthur Miller, *Timebends: A Life* (New York: Grove Press, 1987), p. 228.

3. Ibid., p. 229.

4. Ibid., p. 182.

CHAPTER 9. INTO THE TWENTY-FIRST CENTURY

1. Arthur Miller, *Timebends: A Life* (New York: Grove Press, 1987), p. 546.

2. Ibid., p. 554.

3. Martin Gottfried, *Arthur Miller: His Life and Work* (New York: Da Capo Press, 2003), p. 413.

4. Simi Horwitz, "Arthur Miller: On the Play, Actors and Producers," *Backstage*, November 26, 2003, p. 1.

5. Miller, *Timebends*, p. 599.

GLOSSARY

absurdism—The philosophical and literary doctrine that people live in isolation in a meaningless and nonsensical world.

activism—Practice of vigorous action as a means of achieving political or other ends.

alleviate—To make easier to endure.

combustible—Capable of catching fire.

confederate—An accomplice.

conspirator—A person who takes part in a plot with others.

contrition—Sincere penance or remorse.

crucible—A severe test or trial; a container for burning substances at a high temperature.

despondent—To be depressed or sad.

ecstatic—A state of jubilation or frenzy.

encompass—To include thoroughly.

exonerate—To clear of blame or guilt.

exposition—Writing intended to convey information or explain.

implacable—Not capable of being soothed.

incipient—In an initial stage.

inconsequential—Unimportant.

juxtapose—To place side by side.

lucrative—Moneymaking; profitable.

malicious—Nasty, vicious.

matriarch—The female head of a family.

metaphor—A figure of speech in which a comparison is made between two words or phrases that have no literal relationship.

metaphysical—Concerned with abstract thoughts or subjects beyond the normal senses.

nonrepresentational—Not depicting an object in a recognizable manner.

pivotal—Important; critical to an outcome.

precarious—Unsteady, dangerous.

prestigious—Highly esteemed or honored.

realism—In literature, a manner of treating subject matter that presents a careful, accurate description of everyday life.

requiem—A service, hymn, or dirge for the dead.

retract—To withdraw, take back.

reverberation—Something that is reechoed or reflected.

symbol—Something that stands for, represents, or suggests another thing.

symbolism—The representation of things by use of symbols.

viable—Doable, possible.

voracious—Extremely eager or avid.

MAJOR WORKS BY ARTHUR MILLER

Plays:

The Man Who Had All the Luck (1944)

All My Sons (1947)

Death of a Salesman (1949)

An Enemy of the People (1950) (based on *An Enemy of the People* by Henrik Ibsen)

The Crucible (1953)

A View from the Bridge (1955)

A Memory of Two Mondays (1955)

After the Fall (1964)

Incident at Vichy (1964)

The Price (1968)

The Creation of the World and Other Business (1972)

The Archbishop's Ceiling (1977)

The American Clock (1980)

Two-Way Mirror (1982)

Danger: Memory! (1987)

The Last Yankee (1991)

The Ride Down Mt. Morgan (1991)

Broken Glass (1994)

Mr. Peter's Connections (1998)

Resurrection Blues (2002)

Finishing the Picture (2004)

Film and Television Plays:

The Story of G.I. Joe (1944) (film, uncredited screenplay)

The Misfits (1961) (film based on short story "The Misfits")

Fame (1970) (television play)

Playing for Time (1980) (television play)

Fiction:

Focus (1945) (novel)

I Don't Need You Anymore (1967) (short stories)

Homely Girl (1992) (short stories)

Nonfiction:

Situation Normal (1944)

In Russia (1969)

In the Country (1977)

Chinese Encounters (1979)

Salesman in Beijing (1984)

Timebends (1987) (autobiography)

Collected Essays:

Echoes Down the Corridor (2000)

The Theater Essays of Arthur Miller (2000)

FURTHER READING

Bigsby, Christopher, ed. *The Cambridge Companion to Arthur Miller*. Cambridge: Cambridge University Press, 1997.

Bloom, Harold. *Arthur Miller*. Philadelphia: Chelsea House Publishers, 2003.

Gottfried, Martin. *Arthur Miller: His Life and Work*. New York: Da Capo Press, 2003.

Griffin, Alice. *Understanding Arthur Miller*. Columbia, SC: University of South Carolina Press, 1996.

Siebold, Thomas, ed. *Readings on Death of a Salesman*. San Diego, CA: Greenhaven Press, 1999.

Internet Addresses

The Arthur Miller Society Official Web Site
http://www.ibiblio.org/miller/

An Overview of Arthur Miller's Career
http://curtainup.com/miller.html

***The New York Times* on the Web: Books**
(*Links to reviews and books by and about Arthur Miller*)
http://partners.nytimes.com/books/00/11/12/specials/miller.html

INDEX